FORGOTTEN TRUTH

The Common Vision of the World's Religions

HUSTON SMITH

📖 HarperSanFrancisco

A Division of HarperCollins*Publishers*

Grateful acknowledgment is made for permission to reprint the following material:

Excerpts on pages 94–95 from *Tales of the Dervishes* by Idries Shah. Copyright © 1967 by Idries Shah. Reprinted by permission of Idries Shah and the publishers, Jonathan Cape Ltd., London, England, and E. P. Dutton & Co., Inc.

Excerpts on pages 33 and 145 from "Burnt Norton" and "East Coker" from *Four Quartets* by T. S. Eliot. Reprinted by permission of Harcourt Brace Jovanovich, Inc.

Excerpt on pages 43–46 from *The Monastery of Jade Mountain* by Peter Goullart. Reprinted by permission of John Murray Ltd., London, England.

FIRST HARPERCOLLINS PAPERBACK EDITION PUBLISHED IN 1992

Library of Congress Cataloging-in-Publication Data

Smith, Huston
   Forgotten truth.
   Includes Index
   1. Religion—Philosophy   I. Title
BL51.S572 1985   200'.1
ISBN 0-06-250787-7   92-53925

---

98 ❖/RRD H 10 9 8

CONTENTS

For Eleanor Kendra

ELEANOR: Variant of Helenē (Greek), goddess of light; from *helenē*, "the bright one."

KENDRA: Ken. Scottish, to know; to have perception or understanding.

Kendra. Sanskrit केन्द्र

cognate to the Greek ΚΕΎΤΡΟΥ Center.

Modern society is intensely secular; even those who regret this admit it. The irony is that, after excluding the mystical tradition from our cultural mainstream and claiming to find it irrelevant to our concerns, so many of us feel empty without it.

DAVID MAYBURY-LEWIS, *Millennium*

Preface to the 1992 Edition

People have a profound need to believe that the truth they perceive is rooted in the unchanging depths of the universe; for were it not, could the truth be really important? Yet how can we so believe when others see truth differently? Archaic peoples, wrapped like cocoons in their tribal beliefs, did not face this dilemma. Even civilizations on the whole have been spared it, for until recently they were largely self-contained. It is we— we moderns, we worldly wise—who experience the problem acutely.

This book addresses that problem. Twenty years before it was published in 1976, I wrote *The World's Religions* (originally titled *The Religions of Man*), which presented the major traditions in their individuality and variety. It took me two decades to see how they converge. The outlooks of individual men and women (the militant atheist, the pious believer, the cagey skeptic) are too varied to classify, but when they gather in collectivities—the outlooks of tribes, societies, civilizations, and at deepest level the world's enduring religions—a pattern emerges. One finds a remarkable unity underlying the surface differences. When we look at human bodies we normally notice their external features, which differ markedly. Meanwhile the spines that support this variety are structurally much alike. It is the same with collective outlooks. Outwardly they too differ, but inwardly it is as if an "invisible geometry" has everywhere been working to shape them to a single truth.

The only notable exception is ourselves; our modern Western outlook has differed in its very soul from what might otherwise be called "the human unanimity." But there is an explanation for this, namely, modern science and its misreading. If the cause were science itself, our deviation might be taken as a break-through: a new departure for humankind, the dawning of a new day after a long night of ignorance and superstition. But since the cause has been a misreading of science, our case is an aber-ration. If we correct it we can rejoin the human race.

The time is ripe for that correction—seeing this is what prompts the new Preface to this book. Our mistake was expect-ing science to provide us with a world view, when we now see that it shows us only half the world—its physical, calculable, testable, significantly controllable, half. And even that half is now unpicturable; it can't be visualized (see pages 103–109 in the text). So science no longer presents us with a model for even half of the world. For two thousand years, Europeans followed Aristotle in picturing the earth as surrounded by sentient, crys-talline spheres, a model which modern science displaced with its clockwork universe. Postmodern science gives us not another model of the universe, but no model at all. "Don't ask how na-ture *can* be the way it is," Richard Feynman told his students to-wards the close of his life, "for that question leads down a sink-hole from which no scientist has emerged alive. Nobody has any idea how nature can be the way it is."

So scientific triumphalism, which came close to being mod-ernity's *zeitgeist*, is over, for two reasons. One, we realize that powerful as science is in certain domains, there are other do-mains its empirical method can't track (see pages 14–16 below). Two, the things science can work with no longer converge in a model that makes sense even of nature.

This absence of a model for the world is the deepest defini-tion of postmodernism and the confusion of our times. The two come close to being the same thing. A recent review of eight books, all carrying the word "postmodern" in their titles, throws in the towel, concluding that no one knows what that word means anymore. That's true if we stay with the pundits, but underlying their definitions is a common denominator that is quite serviceable. Ask yourself if you know what's going on. If your answer is no, you're postmodern. "Anyone who isn't confused today," Simone Weil reports, "simply isn't thinking straight."

If people didn't need models of reality and the life-serving orientation and confidence they provide, there would be no problem; but history suggests that we do need them. There have been times when societies were triumphant and became true cultures, when people, through their values and beliefs, knew who they were and were at one with themselves. The *Iliad*, the *Aeneid*, *The Divine Comedy*, *Henry V*, and *War and Peace* celebrate such times. Even in bad times there has usually been a consensus of sorts; symbols had accepted meaning and significance, providing bastions where people could rally, console and entertain themselves, and attack agreed-upon evils. But in our postmodern Western world, as Walker Percy points out, "something has gone wrong, and gone wrong in a sense far more radical than, say, the evils of industrial England which engaged Dickens. It did not take a diagnostician to locate the evils of the sweatshops of the nineteenth-century Midlands. But now it seems that whatever has gone wrong strikes to the heart and core of meaning itself, the very ways [in which] people see and understand themselves." What is called into question now is the very enterprise of human life. Instead of deploring social evils from a posture of consensus, it is now the consensus itself that is called into question. Rebecca West made the point differently while retaining the point itself. Asked to name the mood of this latter twentieth century, she said, "a desperate search for a pattern."

That "the human unanimity"—how things pretty much looked to peoples everywhere until modern science threw the West temporarily off-balance—has helpful things to suggest toward the creation of a viable pattern for our time, is this book's basic thesis. It does not argue foolishly that traditional peoples were, or are, universally wise. Their science has been superseded, and modernity blew the whistle on slavery, even as postmodernity is blowing it on racial and gender injustices. But if somewhere hidden in the depths of things there are invariants—things that resemble the floor of the ocean over which currents sweep, and waves atop those currents—it doesn't much matter when they are pondered, unless (to switch metaphors) one has been in a tunnel so long one has forgotten that sun and stars and rain exist. The premodern realization that they do exist—that things more wonderful than the tunnel vision of modernity allowed are not only real but more real than the ones that pushed them out of sight—is the thesis this essay explores with absolute seriousness.

Four additional points deserve note.

The first concerns the need for twentieth-century science to posit invisible realities, a need that has gathered momentum since this book first appeared. At the opening of the century, William James epitomized religion as "belief that there is an unseen order, and that our supreme good lies in harmoniously adjusting ourselves thereto." In those terms modernity couldn't be wholeheartedly religious, for it looked to science to tell it what existed, and science's silence regarding the unseen rendered distinctive religious objects—God, soul, and the like—suspect. That silence has now lifted; science speaks increasingly of the invisible, and does so respectfully. Ninety percent of the scientist's universe (some say ninety-nine percent) is at present invisible; no instruments pick it up, but calculations require that it be posited to account for the gravitational pull on the rims of galaxies. Instruments may yet be invented that will bring this "dark matter" to light, but even if they are, we will still be left with the wave packets from which particles derive. No scientist expects that those packets will ever be observed.

So science is conceding that invisibles exist, and more. It also concedes that these invisibles precede the visible and create or in some way give rise to it. The aforementioned wave packets attest to this, but if we take the particle, rather than the wave, approach to matter, we get the same result. For protons derive from photons, and photons are only "virtually" material: they have no rest mass, lose no energy to the mediums they traverse, and are not objectively (intersubjectively) detectable because they are annihilated by being perceived. To summarize the way in which science perceives the seen as deriving from the unseen, I will anticipate a short paragraph that appears in larger context on pages 115–16.

> All matter is created out of some imperceptible substratum. This substratum is not accurately described as material, since it uniformly fills all space and is undetectable by any observation. In a sense it appears as nothingness—immaterial, undetectable, and omnipresent. But it is a peculiar form of nothingness, out of which all matter is created.

The second point that deserves mention concerns hierarchies. The multileveled world that this book unfolds may seem to be in tension with critiques of hierarchies that are now healthily afoot, but it is not. For the critique is of social hierarchies, whereas this book deals with metaphysical ones. Metaphysically, all human beings are equal for populating a single level of reality, the human level which Chapters Three and Four place in larger context. Moreover, though social hierarchies *can* be oppressive and often are, not all are of this nature. The hierarchical relationships between loving parents and their small children are benign and empowering; the same may be said of well-ordered classrooms. The basic claim of religion is that God's relation to the world presents us with the paradigmatic instance of a benign, empowering hierarchy. In Christian formulation, "God became man that man might become God" (Athanasius).

Third, it is gratifying to find that my critique of Darwinism (as distinct from evolution) in Chapter Six has gained support since it was written. Those who wish to update themselves on the subject are directed to Phillip E. Johnson's *Darwin on Trial* (Washington, D. C.: Regnery Gateway, 1991); and the booklet, "Evolution as Dogma," published by Haughton Publishing Co., P. O. Box 180218, Dallas, TX 75218–0218.

Finally, overpopulation, the ecological crisis, and other traumas that threaten our very survival. This book does not address them. Not, though, from indifference, but out of the conviction that on their own plane social problems are unsolvable. The causes of social disease, like organic disease, lie deep. Ultimately as deep as the view of our human place in the total scheme of things which this book addresses.

Huston Smith
Berkeley, California
June, 1992

1. THE WAY THINGS ARE

In envisioning the way things are, there is no better place to begin than with modern science. Equally, there is no worse place to end, but that is for later; for now it is the beginning that concerns us. Science is the fitting starting point, partly because of its achievements, which according to Herbert Butterfield outshine everything since the rise of Christianity—others have claimed since the invention of language. Even more pertinent, however, is the fact that science dominates the modern mind. Through and through, from premises to conclusions, the contemporary mind is science-ridden. Its sway is the stronger because we are unaware of its extent.

There may be no better way to summarize the scientific view of things than to say that reality is a stupendous spatial hierarchy, a hierarchy of size. In its middle register, the meso-world in which our daily lives are lived, we encounter objects carrying the proportions of inches, feet, and miles. In the micro-world that undergirds this meso-world, cells measure on the order of thousandths of an inch, atoms hundreds of millionths of an inch, and their nuclei thousandths of billionths of an inch. As we continue downward, or rather inward, from nuclei to nucleons and their ingredient particles, the orders of inverse magnitude continue to unfold exponentially.

Reversing our direction we enter the macro-world. Our sun revolves around our galaxy at a speed of 160 miles per second, about 23 times the speed a rocket must attain to escape from the earth's surface. At this speed it takes the sun approximately

240 million years to complete a single rotation. If the orbit seems large, it is in fact parochial, for it is confined to our own galaxy, which is but one among estimated billions. Andromeda, our closest sizable neighbor, is 2,200,000 light-years away, and beyond it space falls away abysmally, nebula after nebula, island universe after island universe, until we reach the limits of our known universe, some 26 billion light-years "across," whatever that means in a four-dimensional pseudosphere.

Now it happens that the view of reality that preceded that of modern science was likewise hierarchical. Centering in the human plane, it too opened onto higher realms above and nether ones below, the heavens and hells of the traditional cosmologies.

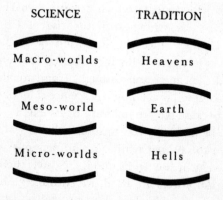

SCIENCE	TRADITION
Macro-worlds	Heavens
Meso-world	Earth
Micro-worlds	Hells

The two views are at one in sharing a hierarchical layout, but the units of measure are different. The scientific gauge is quantity; space, size, and strength of forces can all be reckoned numerically. The comparable "yardstick" in the traditional hierarchy was quality.[1] It had, over the millennia, two distinct

---

1. Language impounds this traditional measure. Dictionaries show that the word "hierarchy" originally designated echelons of angels, the root *hier* meaning "holy."

An alternative word for the traditional yardstick might be "virtue,"

readings that overlapped. To the popular mind it meant essentially euphoria: better meant happier, worse less happy. Reflective minds, on the other hand, considered happiness to be only an aspect of quality, not its defining feature.[2] The word "significance" points us in the direction of the feature they considered fundamental, but significance too was derivative. It was taken for granted that the higher worlds abounded in meaning, significance, and importance, but this was because they were saturated with being and were therefore more real. *Sat, Chit, Ananda:* Being, Awareness, and Bliss. All three pertained, but Being, being basic, came first. In the last analysis, the scale in the traditional hierarchy was ontological.

What it means for one thing to be more real than another will, we trust, become clear as this book proceeds. For the present we note that the view of reality as consisting of graded levels of being dominated man's outlook until the rise of modern science. As we intend to make something of this point, it will be well to fix it into place by documenting it.

With the possible exception of Claude Lévi-Strauss, no one today is more qualified to pronounce on the mentality of precivilized man than is Mircea Eliade. Reducing the ontological hierarchy to its minimum to cover all cases of such men, Eliade finds this minimum to consist in a dichotomy between the sacred and the profane. "The man of the archaic societies tends to live as much as possible *in* the sacred . . . ," he writes, "because for primitives . . . the *sacred* is equivalent to a *power*, and, in the last analysis, to *reality*. The sacred is saturated with *being*."[3]

That which prevailed for tribes carried over into civiliza-

---

with its twin connotations of goodness and power. In Dante's *Divine Comedy*, the planetary heavens and the heaven of fixed stars that surrounds it are pictured as concentric spheres, "all the more vast inasmuch as they possess more virtue."

2. "Better Socrates unhappy than a pig happy." Mill's famous aphorism points up the inability of euphoria to stand as value's final arbiter.

3. Willard Trask, trans., *The Sacred and the Profane* (New York: Harper & Row, 1961), p. 12.

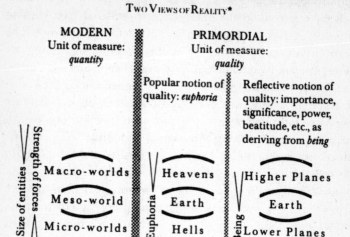

Two Views of Reality*

MODERN
Unit of measure: *quantity*

PRIMORDIAL
Unit of measure: *quality*

Popular notion of quality: *euphoria*

Reflective notion of quality: importance, significance, power, beatitude, etc., as deriving from *being*

Size of entities ← Strength of forces

Macro-worlds
Meso-world
Micro-worlds

Euphoria

Heavens
Earth
Hells

Being

Higher Planes
Earth
Lower Planes

*The alternatives can also be read, roughly, as "scientific vs. humanistic," and "secular vs. sacred."

tions: they refined the hierarchical perspective but kept its basic structure. "It has, in one form or another, been the dominant official philosophy of the larger part of civilized mankind through most of its history," writes Arthur Lovejoy in *The Great Chain of Being* (which along with René Guénon's *Les États Multiples de l'Être* is one of the two studies devoted exclusively to this concept); taught "in their several fashions and with differing degrees of rigor and thoroughness [by] the greater number of subtler speculative minds and of the great religious teachers."[4]

Having noted the universality of the hierarchical perspective in both tribes and civilizations generally, we narrow in on the civilization that is our own. Here, for philosophy, Plato forged the paradigm. Atop being's hierarchy is the Form of the Good,

4. Cambridge: Harvard University Press, 1936, p. 26.

the most real of the various grades of reality, the "Good Itself." Radically different from our everyday world, it can be described only through poetic images. Nevertheless, being "pure perfection," it is the universal object of desire. It is also, of all subordinate things, their cause. Such ancillary and partially privative entities are logically required, Plato's successors (such as Proclus) argued, by virtue of what Lovejoy called "the principle of plenitude"; they are possible, and if any possibility were unactualized it would constitute, as it were, a hole in Being's fullness and negate its infinity. Aristotle elaborated on the graded character of the finite portion of the spectrum;[5] for the *scala naturae* he provided biological specifics and a definition of continuity which came to be applied to the scale as a whole. In the words of Lovejoy's summary:

> The result was the conception of the plan and structure of the world which, through the Middle Ages and down to the late eighteenth century . . . most educated men were to accept without question—the conception of the universe as a "Great Chain of Being," composed of an immense, or . . . infinite, number of links ranging in hierarchical order from the meagerest kind of existents . . . through "every possible" grade up to the *ens perfectissimum*.[6]

"Down to the late eighteenth century," Lovejoy tells us. Why did the hierarchical outlook then collapse? As it had blanketed human history up to that point, constituting man's primordial tradition and what might almost be called the human unanimity, the force that leveled it must have been powerful, and modern science is the obvious candidate. The timing is right: Bacon, Hobbes, and Newton saw the writing on the wall in the seventeenth century, but it took another century for the scientific outlook to sweep the field. And the logic is inexorable: the structure of the two views is such that it was inevitable that they collide. Modern science requires only one

5. "All individual things may be graded according to the degree to which they are infected with potentiality." W. D. Ross, *Aristotle* (London: Methuen, 1949), p. 178.
6. *Great Chain of Being*, p. 59.

ontological level, the physical. Within this level it begins with matter that is perceptible, and to perceptible matter it in the end returns, for however far its hypotheses extend, eventually they must be brought back to pointer readings and the like for verification. Between their beginnings and their ends the hypotheses may cross foreign waters, for in its micro- and macro-reaches matter behaves in unfamiliar ways. This does not, however, alter the fact that the matter (or rather matter/energy) with which the hypotheses deal remains such throughout, subject to matrices of space and time however redefined: curved space is odd, but it is still space. To whatsoever corner of the universe nature is tracked, it continues in some way to honor science's basic indices: space, time, and the matter/energy that are convertible. It is by virtue of the fact that science fits exhaustively into these matrices that its contents are, in last analysis, of a kind. A spatio-temporal state of affairs is a spatio-temporal state of affairs. Or, at a higher level of abstraction, a number is a number, and number is the language of science. Objects can be larger or smaller, forces can be stronger or weaker, durations can be longer or shorter, these all being numerically reckonable. But to speak of anything in science as having a different ontological status—as being better, say, or more real—is to speak nonsense.

Itself occupying no more than a single ontological plane, science challenged by implication the notion that other planes exist. As its challenge was not effectively met, it swept the field and gave the modern world its soul. For this is the final definition of modernity: an outlook in which this world, this ontological plane, is the only one that is genuinely countenanced and affirmed.[7] In religion modernity demythologizes tradition to accommodate it to its one-story universe; if "God" in principle requires more exalted quarters, the nonexistence of such

7. An instance of what we mean: Once while discussing psychic phenomena with Freud, his biographer, Ernest Jones, remarked: "If one could believe in mental processes floating in the air, one could go on to believe in angels." Whereupon Freud closed the discussion with the comment: "Quite so, and even *der liebe Gott*"—even the dear God.

quarters entails his nonexistence as well; hence Death-of-God theologians. Existentialism does its best to give man purchase in a world built for the examination of things, but subjective truth is no match for objective, so in the main philosophy, too, accepts the working premises of science. "The best way to characterize Quine's world view is to say that . . . there is fundamentally only one kind of entity in the world, and that is the kind studied by natural scientists—physical objects; and second, that there is only one kind of knowledge in the world, and it is the kind that natural scientists have."[8] Willard Quine is the most influential American philosopher of the last twenty years.

That the scientific outlook should, in Carl Becker's word, have "ravished" the modern mind is completely understandable. Through technology, science effects miracles: skyscrapers that stand; men standing on the moon. Moreover, in its early stages these miracles were in the direction of the heart's desire: multiplication of goods and the reduction of drudgery and disease. There was the sheer noetic majesty of the house pure science erected, and above all there was method. By enabling men to agree on the truth because it could be demonstrated, this method produced a knowledge that was cumulative and could advance. No wonder man converted. The conversion was not forced. It did not occur because scientists were imperialists but because their achievements were so impressive, their marching orders so exhilarating, that thinkers jostled to join their ranks.

We ourselves were once in their number and would be so today were it not for a fact that has become increasingly unblinkable. Strictly speaking, a scientific world view is impossible; it is a contradiction in terms. The reason is that science does not treat of the world; it treats of a part of it only. One world at a time, one hears. Fair enough, but not half a world, which is all that science can offer.

At this point matters grow awkward, for we are conscious of

8. Richard Schuldenfrei, "Quine in Perspective," *The Journal of Philosophy*, LXIX, 1 (Jan. 13, 1972), 5.

entering upon a hackneyed theme. We beg, however, for the reader's closest attention; we wish he could read the balance of this chapter as if he were encountering its argument for the first time. For its conclusion is one of those things that one knows yet never learns. The conclusion is this: Though man's conversion to the scientific outlook is understandable psychologically, logically it involves a clean mistake. Insofar as we allow our minds to be guided by reason, we can see that to try to live within the scientific view of reality would be like living in a house's scaffolding, and to love it like embracing one's spouse's skeleton.

Every advance in our understanding of the scientific method renders this conclusion more inescapable. Indeed, if there is anything new in the version of the argument about to be presented, it lies in the near-consensus of scientists and philosophers of science that can now be invoked in its support.

As a probe toward the way things are, science is a powerful but strictly limited instrument. One wonders if it was during the Battle of Britain that Karl Popper of the University of London, ranking philosopher of science in our generation, hit upon an image that has become standard in making this point. His image likens science to a searchlight scanning a night sky for planes. For a plane to register, two things are required: it must exist, and it must be where the beam is. The plane must *be*, and it must be *there* (where the beam is).

The point of this image is, of course, to make plain the restricted nature of the scientific quest. Far from lighting up the entire sky, it illumines but an arc within it. Norbert Wiener used to make the point by saying: "Messages from the universe arrive addressed no more specifically than 'To Whom It May Concern.' Scientists open those that concern them." No mosaic constructed from messages thus narrowly selected can be the full picture.

These images make their point in a general way, but they provide no particulars. Precisely *how* is science limited? In what ways does it restrict its interests?

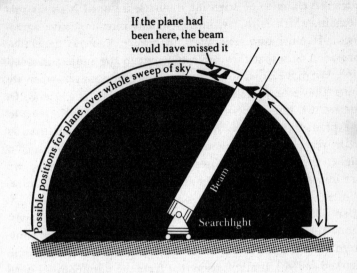

Science is not one thing. It resembles a village more than it does a single individual. But villages often have greens, and they are usually located near their centers. Following this analogy, we can move in on science by way of a series of concentric circles.

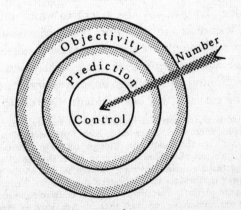

The outer, enveloping circle is labeled *objectivity*. No knowledge can claim to be scientific in any sense until it enters this domain, which is to say, until it elicits intersubjective agreement. It must commend itself to human knowers generally, provided only that they are competent in the subject in question. We move closer to the heart of science, however, when we enter the second circle, *prediction*. Taxonomy is a science in some sense, but it does not command the respect we accord to the predictive sciences. When an astronomer tells us that so many years hence, at such and such an hour on such and such a night, the moon will enter eclipse, and this happens, we are impressed. Not content to describe what occurs in nature, the astronomer has pressed on to uncover its operators. A scientist who goes further and takes command of these operators, throwing switches in the tracks on which nature runs, so to speak, steps even closer to science's center, into the circle marked *control*. It might seem that from the standpoint of pure as against applied science the distinction between prediction and control is small, but in fact it is important. In pure science controlled experiments set the stage for predictions that could not be made without them—science grows exact by being exacting—while in applied science (technology) control is where the money lies. It is to the science that can build missile systems and stamp out polio that the coffers of government swing wide. To overlook the extent to which this affects the shape of science as a sociohistorical enterprise would be naïve.[9]

The fourth guideline of science takes the form, not of another circle that hugs its center even more tightly, but of an arrow which, beginning at the outer rim, drives straight to the center itself. The name of this final guideline is *number*.[10] Number,

9. Science is the controlled observation of nature, technology its controlled exploitation. Heidegger calls both "provocative" and sees "self" and "control" as the dominant, though concealed, motifs not only of modern science but of the basic notion of truth that develops in the West. Nietzsche anticipated him in seeing modern science as the product of the will to power that animates all Western thought and history.

10. Or more precisely, mathematics, which embraces the study of relationships that are numerical and ones that are not, such as "greater/smaller,"

as has already been remarked, is the language of science; the more knowledge can be expressed quantitatively, in probability equations and the like, the more scientific it is considered to be.[11] The question of whether the social sciences will achieve the status of true sciences turns on this point, with economics being, at present, the test case.

It will be objected that this fourfold characterization presents science in its narrowest light. There is much talk today of expanding the scientific method to make it applicable to broader, more humane considerations. By directing this method to new problems, the scientific *enterprise* can indeed, within limits, be expanded, but not the scientific method itself. For it is precisely from the narrowness of that method that its power derives, so that to urge its expansion is like recommending that a dentist's drill be broadened so it can churn a bit of butter on the side.[12] We are at liberty, of course, to use

---

"coincides with/does not coincide with," "falls within this set/does not so fall," these latter being the preserve of mathematical logic. It is in this inclusive sense of mathematics that Whitehead writes, "All science as it grows toward perfection becomes mathematical in its ideal."

11. This point was first brought home to me through a chance conversation while I was teaching at the Massachusetts Institute of Technology. Lunching at its Faculty Club, I found myself seated next to a scientist, and as so often happened in such circumstances the conversation turned to the difference between science and the humanities. We were getting nowhere when suddenly he broke in on something I was saying with the authority of a man who had discovered Truth. "I have it!" he exclaimed. "The difference between us is that I count and you don't."

The key differences between the primordial and contemporary perspectives in a double entendre.

12. In *Where the Wasteland Ends*, Theodore Roszak calls for "changing the fundamental sensibility of scientific thought—and doing so even if we must drastically revise the professional character of science and its place in our culture." He proposes a science that is dominated by a "rhapsodic intellect" which "would subordinate much research to those contemplative encounters with nature that deepen, but do not increase knowledge" (Garden City, N.Y.: Doubleday & Co., 1972), pp. 374–75.

To which a practicing scientist rightly replies: "My answer is that science cannot change in this way without destroying itself, because however much human values are involved in the scientific process or are affected by the results of scientific research, there is an essential element in science that is cold, objective, and nonhuman." Steven Weinberg, "Reflections of a Working Scientist," *Daedalus*, CIII, 3 (Summer 1974), 42.

words as we please, and "science" is no exception. We can even revert to its scholastic definition wherein theology is science's queen—would the proponents of an expanded science like this definition better? The hope is only that Confucius will be honored in his call for "the rectification of names," his plea that when we use words we understand and make plain what we are doing with them. Underlying much of the call for an expanded science is a stifled cry: "Please, in this age of science, believe me, too, the way scientists are believed," or "Please consider my research proposal eligible for funding by the National Science Foundation, whose budget is many times that of the National Endowment on the Arts and the Humanities." But we need not resort to *ad hominems*. For all we know, the larger part of the motive for trying to expand science is not self-serving; it is merely mistaken. The idealistic element in it is its desire to achieve in the understanding of man what science has achieved in the understanding of matter. Its mistake is in not seeing that the tools for the one are of strictly limited utility for the other, and that the practice of trying to see man as an object which the tools of science *will* fit leads first to underrating and then to losing sight of his attributes those tools miss. (Pages of illustrations, but the mere titles of B. F. Skinner's *Beyond Freedom and Dignity* and Herbert Marcuse's *One-Dimensional Man* will, in opposite ways, suffice.) If it be asked, "But what did the nonscientific approach to man and the world give us?" the answer is: "Meaning, purpose, and a vision in which everything coheres." But we are getting ahead of our story.

We were speaking of numbers, and the subject warrants a second small excursus before we leave it. Why numbers work as they do with nature—or to put the matter the other way around, why nature is as mathematical as it has proven to be —no one fully understands. Eugene Wigner speaks of "the unreasonable effectiveness of mathematics"; it is a mystery sufficient to awaken the Pythagorean in us all. One of the reasons for mathematics' effectiveness, however, we do know. Numbers and their logical operators are the only symbols, or rather signs, that are completely unambiguous: 4 is 4 and that is the end of the matter. This alone could account for why scientists press in their direction, for whatever else science seeks, it seeks precision.

One can sense a problem brewing here, for if number is the vehicle of precision (major premise), and number is not the unit of measure in tradition (minor premise), whose basic measure is quality rather than quantity, does it not follow (conclusion) that the traditional outlook is forever and in principle condemned to vagueness? As far as descriptions of that outlook are concerned, and insofar as these descriptions are compared with scientific descriptions, the answer must be yes; the syllogism is valid. But lest it be concluded that this difference closes the books on the traditional perspective, we must register immediately that tradition's limitations in the direction of precision carry compensations. The alternative to numbers is words. Whereas numbers are signs, words are symbols, and therefore by their very nature equivocal; their ambiguity can be reduced but never eliminated. This bars them from the needle's eye of absolute precision, but the loose ends that prevent them from piercing that eye endow them with a texture that numbers cannot match. Multivalent, irreducibly equivocal in intimation and nuance where not actually ambiguous in dictionary definition, words reach out like a banyan root system, as tangled and in as many directions. Folding and refolding in adumbration and allusion, they weave, veer, and seek out subliminal soil. No wonder logicians flee their meanderings in favor of fixed and adamantine glyphs. The despair of logicians is the humanist's glory. From the adversity of verbal ambiguity, opportunity opens. The multivalence of language enables it to mesh with the multidimensionality of the human spirit, depicting its higher reaches as numbers never can.[13] Equations

13. Exceptions to this statement are numerologists and "gnostic mathematicians" for whom numbers function as symbols reflecting another realm. Pythagoras was such, as were certain members of Plato's Academy who, by Aristotle's report, claimed that "the Forms are numbers."

That type is exceptional, but another point relating to the number/words distinction is of general interest. In the chapter on "Information" in his

can be elegant, but that is a separate matter. Poems cannot be composed in numbers.

We are now in a position to see how science is limited. The knowledge with which it is exclusively occupied is, to begin with, objective. It must be intersubjectively confirmable, and since sense data are what men most incontrovertibly agree on after the tautologies of mathematics and logic, the knowledge science seeks is that which at some level of amplification can connect with man's senses. That which so connects is energy/matter, so energy/matter in its manifold forms and permutations *is* science's object. Within its domain science looks especially for precise—which in the end means mathematically expressible—knowledge that is predictive and augments control.

What lies outside this pale?

1. *Values in their final and proper sense.* Some time ago Bertrand Russell acknowledged that "the sphere of values lies outside science, except insofar as science consists in the pursuit of knowledge,"[14] and even his exception is not truly such, for the value of pursuing knowledge, though assumed by science, is not itself scientifically derived. Science can deal with instrumental values but not intrinsic ones. *If* health is valued over immediate somatic gratification, smoking is bad, but the "if"

Lives of a Cell, Lewis Thomas cites ambiguity as the property that distinguishes language from other modes of biological communcation:

> Ambiguity seems to be an essential, indispensible element for the transfer of information from one place to another by words, where matters of real importance are concerned. It is often necessary, for meaning to come through, that there be an almost vague sense of strangeness and askewness. Speechless animals and cells cannot do this. . . . Only the human mind is designed to work in this way, programmed to drift away in the presence of locked-on information, straying from each point in a hunt for a better, different point" (Toronto: Bantam Books, 1974), p. 111.

Language is biological in that we are programmed to learn it, Dr. Thomas concludes, but it is peculiar in being a "programming for ambiguity," to put the matter in the paradox his point requires.

For the present book, which warns against over-reliance on a mode of knowing that favors monovalent numbers over multivalent words, the point is big with consequences.

14. "Science and Values," in Philip Wiener, ed., *Readings in the Philosophy of Science* (New York: Charles Scribner's Sons, 1953), p. 599.

itself science cannot adjudicate. Again, science can deal with values descriptively but not prescriptively. It can tell us what men do prize, but not what they should prize. Market research and opinion polls are sciences, but as the word is used today there can be no science of the *summum bonum*. Normative values elude its grasp.

2. *Purposes*. For science to get on with its job, Aristotle's final causes had to be banished and the field cleared for explanation in terms of efficient causes alone. Whether the case be that of Galileo and falling stones or Kepler and light, the shift "from the mechanics of antiquity to modern mechanics [comes through] the . . . separation of primary and secondary qualities, . . . the numerical and affective aspects of nature, . . . to remove the language of volition and teleology, and to fortify the notion of 'impersonal,' causal laws of motion."[15] Vitalism is unscientific. Behavioral science traces "purposive behavior" to instincts and conditioning, à la B. F. Skinner; biology tracks tropisms to the codings of genes or chromosomes, à la Monod's *Chance and Necessity*. It is "feedback loops" that render organisms "teleonomic." "The cornerstone of scientific method is . . . the *systematic* denial that 'true' knowledge can be got at by interpreting phenomena in terms of final causes—that is to say, of 'purpose.' "[16]

3. *Life meanings*. Science itself is meaningful from beginning to end, but on certain kinds of meanings—ones that are existential and global—it is silent. What is the meaning of our days? Does life make sense? Does the cosmic drama have point and purpose? As a human being, a scientist may become engaged with such questions, but his science will not help him answer them.[17] It is as if as scientist he were situated inside a balloon. He can shine his flashlight anywhere on its interior,

15. Gerald Holton, "The Roots of Complementarity," *Daedalus*, XCIX, 4 (Autumn 1970), 1023.

16. Jacques Monod, *Chance and Necessity* (New York: Vintage Books, 1972), p. 21.

17. Even in the period in which scientific propositions enjoyed pride of place in his philosophy, Wittgenstein acknowledged that they leave "the problems of life . . . completely untouched" (*Tractatus*, 6.52).

but he cannot get outside it to see it as a whole or in perspective.

4. *Quality.* This is basic to the lot, for it is the qualitative ingredient in values, meanings, and purposes that accounts for their power. Certain qualities (such as colors) are connected with quantifiable substrates (lightwaves of given lengths), but quality itself is unmeasurable.[18] Either it is perceived for what it is or it is not, and nothing can convey its nature to anyone who cannot perceive it directly. The most that one can do is to compare things that have a quality with things that do not, and even then the comparison is meaningful only to persons who know from experience what the quality in question is. Inability to deal with the qualitatively unmeasurable leads science to work with what Lewis Mumford calls "a disqualified universe."

Values, life meanings, purposes, and qualities slip through science like sea slips through the nets of fishermen. Yet man swims in this sea, so he cannot exclude it from his purview. This is what was meant when we noted earlier that a scientific *world* view is in principle impossible. Taken in its entirety, the world is not as science says it is; it is as science, philosophy, religion, the arts, and everyday speech say it is. Not science but the sum of man's symbol systems, of which science is but one, is the measure of things.

With science itself there can be no quarrel. Scientism is another matter. Whereas science is positive, contenting itself with reporting what it discovers, scientism is negative. It goes beyond the actual findings of science to deny that other approaches to knowledge are valid and other truths true. In doing so it deserts science in favor of metaphysics—bad metaphysics, as it happens, for as the contention that there are no truths save those of science is not itself a scientific truth, in affirming it scientism contradicts itself. It also carries marks of a religion—a secular religion, resulting from overextrapolation

18. Augustine noted the distinction with respect to time. "For so it is, O Lord, my God, I measure it, but what it is I measure I do not know."

from science, that has seldom numbered great scientists among its votaries. Science has enormous difficulty dealing with things that cannot be measured (if it can deal with them at all), yet David Bohm, who *is* a great scientist, says that "the immeasurable is the primary and independent source of all reality. . . . Measure is a secondary and dependent aspect of this reality."[19]

Where are we?

Searching for the way things are, we found that the modern reduction of reality to a single ontological level was the result of science. But its psychological, not its logical, result; this was our further finding. Nothing in what science has discovered controverts the existence of realms other than the one with which it deals. Meanwhile our growing understanding of the scientific method shows us that there are things science by-passes. Whether these neglected items belong to a distinct ontological scale, science, of course, does not say; it says nothing whatever about them. The fact that scientific instruments do not pick them up shows only that they differ in *some* way from the data science does register.

As long as modernity was captive of an outlook presumed to be scientific but in fact scientistic, reality was taken to be as science mirrored it. Now that it is apparent that science peers down a restricted viewfinder, we are released from that misconception. The view that appears in a restricted viewfinder is a restricted view.

Since reality exceeds what science registers, we must look for other antennae to catch the wavebands it misses. What other antennae are there? None more reliable than the convergent sensibilities of, in Lovejoy's characterization, "the greater number of the subtler speculative minds and of the great religious teachers" that civilizations have produced; and, we have added with Eliade, that archaic societies have produced as well. Lovejoy's crediting of the hierarchical outlook to the

19. *Journal of the Blaisdell Institute*, IX, 2 (1974), 70.

subtler of human minds gains force from the fact that, writing as he did in the heyday of scientism, he thought the hierarchical outlook mistaken. When we combine (a) the fact that it has been the subtler minds which, when not thrown off balance by the first flush of the scientific breakthrough, have gravitated to the hierarchical view, with (b) the further fact that, from the multiple heavens of Judaism to the storied structure of the Hindu temple and the angelologies of innumerable traditions, the view was reached convergently and independently, as if by innate tropism, by virtually all known societies; when, to repeat, we combine these two facts and bring them into alignment, they entitle us to regard a tiered reality as man's central surmise when the full range of his experience is legitimated and pondered profoundly. Constituting until recently, through both rumored and recorded history, what we have ventured to call the human unanimity—the phrase overstates the case slightly, but not much—it presents itself as the natural human outlook: the view that is normal to man's station because consonant with the complete complement of human sensibilities. It is the vision philosophers have dreamed, mystics have seen, and prophets have transmitted.

> Spatial metaphors are always dangerous, though unavoidable, in Theology. In space if A is touching B then B must be touching A. In the spiritual world this is not so. God is near me (or rather *in* me), and yet I may be far from God because I may be far from my own true self.
>
> C. E. ROLT, Introduction to Dionysius the Areopagite, *The Divine Names and The Mystical Theology*

> Tell the truth, but tell it slant.
>
> EMILY DICKINSON

2. Symbolism of Space: The Three-Dimensional Cross

A misunderstanding dogs the view of reality as multi-leveled which, if not dispelled, will vitiate everything that follows. Levels imply space, space entails distance, and distance spells separation. But separation is what religion seeks to over-come. Does it not follow that a hierarchical ontology which splits reality into a number of discrete levels builds cleavage into the very structure of existence and thereby makes endemic the disease religion seeks to cure? Reasonings of this sort appear to be widespread. How else are we to account for the attention an Anglican bishop received for his midlife discovery that God is not "out there"? We refer to the reception accorded John Robinson's *Honest to God*.

Actually, there is a sense in which God emphatically *is* "out there." In his power and awe-filled majesty he is *ganz anders,* radically other, infinitely removed from what we are and thereby "high as the heaven is above the earth." Concomitantly, of course, he is "nearer than our jugular vein," "closer to us than breathing, nearer than hands and feet," for "in him we live and move and have our being." In Augustine's plain words, "It is arrant nonsense that the soul is without Him who is everywhere." Transcendence *and* immanence, in absolute tension. If we lose our grip on either, the tone in our spiritual life collapses.

The reception Bishop Robinson's book received was the lay aftermath of the reception theologians had themselves for a generation accorded Rudolf Bultmann's move to "demythologize" Christian cosmology of its three-storied universe. Both evince a surprising innocence regarding religious symbols and the way they function. One of the reasons a hierarchical view of reality is indispensable is that Spirit, the human spirit included, is nonspatial and thereby belongs perforce to an order of existence distinct in kind from nature. It follows that no spatial, geographical terms—out there, deep within, high and lifted up, basic, fundamental, exalted, whatever—can characterize Spirit literally. But as an epigraph at the head of this chapter notes, neither can such terms be avoided. Insofar as we think, spatial images are inevitable, for thought proceeds through language, and language is forged in our encounter with the spatio-temporal world.

Envisioned externally, as residing outside of man and apart from him, the Good dons metaphors of height: "I shall lift up mine eyes unto the hills . . . "; "in the year that King Uzziah died, I saw the Lord, high and lifted up." When man reverses his gaze and looks inward, his value-imagery likewise transposes; it turns over. Within man, the best lies deepest; it is basic, fundamental, the ground of his being. All the levels of reality are within man, for microcosm mirrors macrocosm; man mirrors the Infinite. But mirrors invert; hence symbolism's "law of inverse analogy."[1] That which man seeks exter-

1. If the reader objects that mirrors reverse right/left but not up/down, he should read Ned Block, "Why Do Mirrors Reverse Right/Left but Not Up/Down?" *The Journal of Philosophy*, LXXI, 9 (May 16, 1974), 259 ff. The written page which a mirror reverses right/left has been *turned*

nally in the highest heavens he seeks internally in the depths of his soul. Spiritual space, like physical, is curved. We journey far to reach our origin.

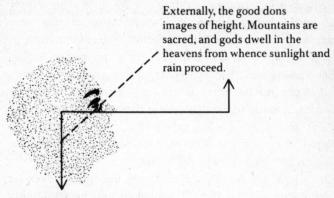

Externally, the good dons images of height. Mountains are sacred, and gods dwell in the heavens from whence sunlight and rain proceed.

Internally, the good dons images of depth. We sense it as centered, like the heart and other vital organs, within a protective sheath of bone and sinew.

We trust that this brief note on the symbolism of space removes what would otherwise be an insuperable obstacle to the concept of an hierarchical reality. Its higher levels are not literally elsewhere; they are removed only in the sense of being inaccessible to ordinary consciousness—invisible, for one thing. In this respect the multiple states of being resemble multiple dimensions more than they do multiple levels. If space has indeed a fourth dimension—we are not referring to time—that dimension is not elsewhere; it intersects the three dimensions we see, albeit invisibly. The imagery of dimensions

---

right/left, not upside down, to face the mirror. This is only the beginning of the complexities that reflected vision presents, but for present purposes these are irrelevant. Quite apart from mirrors, the image that is filtered to the retina through the eye's lens is already inverted, practice being required for us to compensate for that fact and "see" the image as upright.

has the further advantage of underscoring the ontological differences at issue. Distance can render things invisible and this the imagery of levels allows, but something that is invisible while being right under one's nose, not because it is covered or microscopic but because we lack the kind of sense receptors that could connect with it—a something of this sort is intrinsically mysterious. Science fiction writers know this: good science fiction is set on other planets, great science fiction in other dimensions. For to repeat, the notion of dimensions beyond our normal three is uncanny from the outset, before anything is made to happen within them. In its preoccupation with a "more" that exceeds man's ken, science fiction is kin to religion, the emphatic difference, of course, being that what is fiction for one is for the other fact.

In view of the double advantage of dimensions over levels —the advantage that dimensions, when multiplied, announce domains that are (a) inherently awe-filled while being (b) directly at hand—we might be tempted to adopt them as our controlling spatial metaphor. To do so, however, would be a mistake, for the simple reason that dimensions lack a value gradient. Length is not better than breadth, breadth than height, or whatever. Rather than being distributed across spatial dimensions, value differences fall along a single one, the vertical. Better and worse are not left and right; they are superior and inferior. And because the comparative worth of existences is crucial to our concerns, the imagery of levels is on balance more appropriate.

It is more appropriate for ordering domains with respect to their worth, but to symbolize existence in its entirety all three dimensions are needed. When St. Paul hoped that the Christians of Ephesus would be filled with the fullness of God, he prayed that they would be granted power to comprehend "the breadth and length, and depth and height" of Christ's love (Eph. 3:18), for only so could they know its inclusiveness. Our special concern is with the height aspect of his formulation, but to see how worth figures in being as a whole we need to use the symbolism of the other dimensions as well.

René Guénon's *Symbolism of the Cross* must be credited for much that we are about to say.[2]

No model is more effective in disclosing the symbolism that is latent in space than a three-dimensional cross, constituted of a vertical cross pierced at its intersection by a third, longitudinal arm running at right angles to the other two. The construct can also be seen as deriving from the imposition of a horizontal cross on a vertical one, in which case the model symbolizes not only reality—its meaning that concerns us here —but also, in passing, the meeting of East and West, for the Asian counterpart of the upright Christian cross is one that is typically inscribed on the ground. Such a horizontal cross is a mandala, a sacred enclosure, round or square, with typically four approaches to a "hidden treasure" that lies at its center. The diagram is, of course, universal: the Garden of Eden with its four rivers converging on the Tree of Life at its center is a mandala, as is the New Jerusalem in the Book of Revelation with its twelve gates—small entrances flanking each of the four principal ones are common in mandalic layouts. But though mandalas cover the globe, Asia has worked with them more intensively than has the West. Often they are paintings that are hung on walls, but their basic position in Asia is, to repeat, horizontal, as in the ground plans of Angkor Wat and the stupa at Boroboedoer, the room-size butter mandalas the Tibetans build for feast days, or the patterns Indian women inscribe on floors and courtyards with rice flour. Pare such a horizontal mandala to its essential geometry of two lines that intersect at right angles and mount this horizontal cross on a vertical, Christian cross to make one having six arms like the "pickup jacks" that children play with; the vertical cross should be of Eastern Orthodox design so the six arms can be of equal length and the center truly central. The result is a three-dimensional cross, the most adequate model of reality that space can provide.

Let us begin with its vertical axis. As the *axis mundi* it

2. London: Luzac & Company, 1958.

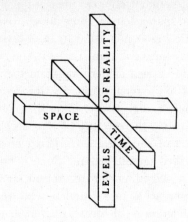

intersects all the planes of existence and ranks them in ontological hierarchy, the hierarchy of being and worth. Of the planes thus traversed, our model shows but one, the one represented by its horizontal arms. This is as it should be, for our own plane is the only one we can see. But if we possessed metaphysical eyes we would see arms protruding from all the points the vertical axis registers.

How many planes there are, we do not know. The levels of nature that science discriminates give us no clue, for these all pertain to size which, being an aspect of space, belongs to our plane only. (We discount as irrelevant for present purposes the peculiar modes of space we experience when dreaming.) The entire size-continuum, from minutest particle to our 26-billion-light-year universe, falls along the horizontal arms we see. The planes that bracket this central one—central from our point of view—may be indefinite in number, but even if they are, something can be said about their antipodes. As the levels of reality array themselves along the vertical axis in descending degrees of reality, reality being (as noted in the

preceding chapter) worth's final criterion, the bottom of the
arm represents the point—a fraction of a degree above absolute
zero as we might say—where being phases out completely; all
that could lie beyond this margin is a nothing that is as un-
thinkable as it is nonexistent. The top of the axis represents
the opposite of this, that is, everything. Opposites being well
acquainted, this everything shares in common with its anti-
thesis the fact that it too cannot be imaged, but unlike
complete nothingness it can be conceived. Being we experience, whereas nothingness, by itself, we do not. The zenith of
being is Being Unlimited, Being relieved of all confines and
conditionings. The next chapter will discuss it; for now we
simply name it. It is All-Possibility, the Absolute, the In-finite
in all the directions that word can possibly point.

Returning to the horizontal arms that denote the human
plane, the transverse or lateral arm represents space and by
extension the amplitude of possibilities it can contain. The
longitudinal arm, in turn—the one that extends toward the
viewer and away from him—represents time; from its center,
the present, its stretches backward toward an indefinite past
and forward toward an open and unlimited future. Inching
forward along this longitudinal arm with time's passage, the
lateral arm represents at each point all the possibilities that
could in principle transpire at that moment in time on our
particular plane of existence. If we could see the past and the
future, lateral arms would spring from every point on the
longitudinal line and convert the horizontal arms of the cross
into a plane. And if to such time-consciousness were added the
metaphysical omniscience posited earlier—the capacity to perceive all the levels of being that exist—we would see that the
horizontal, space-time plane is only a section of a cube. Or
rather, because a circle encloses more space for the length of its
perimeter than does a square and amplitude is our object, a
sphere does better than a cube as our final image for being's
totality.

From the infinite sphere toward which the arms of the cross

point, let us now contract our attention to the center from which the arms protrude. In intersecting at this center the arms symbolize resolution, a principle which for spiritual existence is decisive.

Two kinds of resolution are represented. The first of these is *the union of complements*. Things that are complementary differ from each other, and the differences can produce tensions and even open warfare. But the differences can also "come together," as the convergence of the horizontal and vertical arms indicates. In intersecting, the arms of the vertical cross form, as it were, a Western yin-yang. The vertical line represents most obviously the male or active principle and the horizontal line the female, receptive one, but any complementing aspects of existence can be substituted. Complements differ illimitably; this fact the arms register by diverging at right angles with their extremities moving increasingly apart. They need not be at odds, however, for at base—in the mathematical point where they intersect—they are identical.

If the intersection of the horizontal and vertical axes of the vertical cross represents the union of complements, the meeting of the right and left arms of its horizontal axis represents *the resolution of opposites*. The horizontal and vertical axes form a right angle, but the angle formed by the outbranchings of the two halves of the horizontal axis is 180 degrees. In protruding in directions that are diametrically opposed, these halves represent alternatives that are irreconcilable: forced options, excluded middles, dilemmas with horns on them, decisions that are either/or. Complements can coexist, and the problem is how to harmonize them; opposites are exclusive, and the problem is which to choose. Monogamous or polygamous; one may be either but not both simultaneously. Choices of this kind can be agonizing, as the tension in the thrusts of the right and left arms illustrates; they can tear a man apart. But at the point from which left and right diverge, this tension too is stilled, the message being that insofar as one leads a centered life, tensions disappear. Aristotelian contradictories do indeed preclude a middle, but the converse of this truth is that when the middle appears, contradictories cease to be such. Their logical exclusiveness may remain, but the existential tension goes out of them. "Oppositions . . . cease to affect the being who has reduced his ego to nothing" (*Tao Te Ching*).

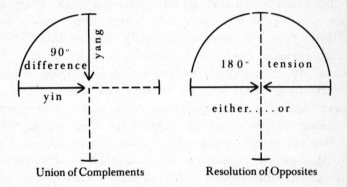

Union of Complements   Resolution of Opposites

Existentially, then, the cross's center represents the point where complements unite and opposites are resolved. Meanwhile ontologically it is the "here and now" from which time and space protrude. Clearly this point merits attention.

All space condenses into the mathematical point. Collapsed successively, a three-dimensional cube becomes a two-dimensional plane, a two-dimensional plane a one-dimensional line, a one-dimensional line a mathematical point. By the same token, all space proceeds from the mathematical point. Its movement in a single direction produces a line; movement of this line at right angles to itself produces a plane; movement of the plane at right angles to itself produces a cube. Geometry derives from the mathematical point.

But this brings us to something interesting. Source of all space, the mathematical point is itself spaceless. The smallest unit of space is not the Euclidean point which, as a position without dimensions, occupies no space whatever. The smallest distance possible is the distance between two such points that are immediately adjacent; smaller than this is no distance whatever. Extension is the expanse between two simultaneously existing points, but the points themselves are not parts of the spatial continuum, though the distance they "produce" requires that they be conceived as situated within space. The true spatial element is not the point but distance.

Symbolically this is exact, for the human plane, woven of space, derives from a transworldly source where space is not. Asked if there is life after death, Martin Buber replied, "There is no after, for time is but a crystallization in the mind of God." Space as well. Space derives from nonspace, if this expression does not seem too peculiar and unusual. "Out of that which is not, He made that which is. He carved great columns from the impalpable ether" (The Kabbalah). Equally —this was Buber's point—time derives from nontime. The six days of creation correspond to the six arms of our cross. On the seventh day God returns to the point from which his actions began. On the seventh day he rested.

This brings us back to the vertical axis of the cross, which registers degrees of reality, for something that is aloof from space and time, eluding both their confines and their separations, obviously exceeds the world our senses report. In the next chapter the higher planes of reality will occupy us in some detail, but for the present we need note only the one at the top. The supreme plane from which the vertical axis descends is the Infinite: Being exempt from every mode of limitation and restriction. From this pinnacle all lesser being derives. We can picture the vertical axis as a line which, tapping into the infinite reservoir of Being at its summit, transmits a portion of its store to the subordinate planes, which by dint of this transfusion "materialize." Each successively lower plane receives a smaller allotment, not because Being becomes progressively depleted—the reservoir, we recall, is infinite—but because every grade of finitude must be actualized. Were any omitted, they would gape as holes, so to speak, depriving existence of the completeness the Infinite requires by name and possesses in fact. In alternative imagery the conduit is the Celestial Ray of the world's mythologies, connecting the sun to each entity in the universe it illumines. Geometrically the vertical axis is a mathematical line which, having no width, intersects the human plane through the mathematical point in the cross's center. Through this point which, being space-less, is unimplicated in the world it empowers, there flows from the Infinite the measure of being that is earth's allotment. In the act of flooding the human plane, being dons the categories we know: space, time, and matter. And this is the meaning of our earth's existence: to actualize reality in its own dis-tinctive fashion, according to its allotted categories. For this middling mode of existence—partly real, partly not—is pos-sible, and being possible must *be*, that the scheme of things be truly entire.

If we may postulate a microsecond preceding the moment with which the astronomers' story begins—the moment some 13 billion years ago when a superdense kernel of matter began the explosion that they say is still creating our universe—the natural order may literally have derived from a mathe-matical point at its core.[3] Be this as it may, the metaphysical origin of the physical universe as recounted in the preceding paragraphs is paralleled by the origination of the human soul. As without, so within; the man/world isomorphism which we shall note repeatedly in this study swings again into view. For the point at the center of the three-dimensional cross that gives rise to the order of nature concomitantly creates the souls that inhabit that order, not just in the moment of their conception but continuously, instant by instant as they pursue their trajectories. Or to speak more precisely (and in doing so to anticipate two chapters hence), the mathematical point at the center of the three-dimensional cross is likewise each soul's

3. "The universe did not necessarily begin with the big bang. . . . *Our* universe, however, did begin with the primordial explosion, since we can obtain no information about events that occurred before it." David Schramm, "The Age of the Elements," *Scientific American*, CCXXX, 1 (Jan. 1974), 70.

center.[4] If it strikes the reader as presumptuous to equate his personal center with the center of the cosmos, he must be reminded that physics requires him to do just that; because space is relative and curved, the center of the physical universe is for each observer the point from which his observations proceed. If, still incredulous, still resisting the notion that the center of his self is in some way identical with that of creation at large—have we not learned the lesson of Copernicus?—the reader continues to try to position himself marginally by arguing that a single center cannot occupy 4 billion bodies simultaneously, he forgets that the spatial distinctions he has introduced have no bearing on the mathematical point which, as we have seen, produces space without being implicated in it. The Hermetic formulation is exact: "God is a sphere whose center is everywhere and circumference nowhere." At the top of the mountain Black Elk reported that he was at the center of the universe. "But," he added, "that center is everywhere." According to Buddhism, there is a Buddha in every grain of sand.

As the all-empowering but impalpable essence that creates each snowflake of existence and causes it to settle in its own proper place, the mathematical point is in everything. Kabbalists call it the Inward or Holy Palace; in Islam it is the Divine Station that combines contrasts and antinomies. In

4. "Know the embodied soul to be a part of the hundredth part of the point of a hair divided a hundred times; and yet it is infinite." Svetasvatara Upanishad, V.9.

This juxtaposition of the infinitesimal and the infinite underscores the fact that symbols, being fragmentary, can never capture more than an aspect of their referents. What escapes the symbol of the mathematical point is the truth that it is infinitely greater than the selves and universe that derive from it. "It therefore needs to be complemented at the back of our minds by another circle whose center stands for this world and whose circumference symbolizes the All-Surrounding Infinite." Martin Lings, *What Is Sufism?* (Berkeley: University of California Press, 1975), p. 22—see figure on p. 61 below. Meister Eckhart invokes the symbolism of this second circle when he writes: "The soul that enters into God owns neither time nor space. . . . But it stands to reason, if you consider it, that the space occupied by any soul is vastly greater than heaven and earth and God's entire creation. I say more: God might make heavens and earths galore yet these . . . would be of less extent than a single needle-tip compared with the standpoint of a soul atoned in God."

China it is the Chung Yung, the Invariable Middle, the Taoist Void that unites the spokes and makes of them a wheel. Though nothing could exist without it, in the realm of the Ten Thousand Things only man can be aware of it and identify with it intentionally. The awareness can be cultivated directly through meditation or indirectly through the "meditation of everyday life," which aims at reducing the tension between the contraries of human existence. Practicing detachment, the aspirant undercuts the vicissitudes of the stream of forms and attains peace in emptiness. To connote the point where the opposites of space and time are resolved, Blake wrote of "infinity in the palm of your hand / And eternity in an hour"; the phrase "holy indifference," for its part, tokens the fact that in that selfsame point the opposition between good and evil likewise collapses:

> One to me is fame and shame,
> One to me is loss and gain;
> One to me is pleasure, pain.
>
> *Bhagavad-Gita*

Passage through the "gateless gate" (Mu Mon Kan) that guards the holy center can be disorienting. If it takes the form of a powerful satori it can feel as if one has been sucked into a "black hole" where physical laws are destroyed. When eyes have accustomed themselves to the new, ethereal light, however, one sees that no movement has occurred. Length and breadth had already withdrawn into the cross's horizontal center; now the vertical axis too collapses. Renouncing the space it had embodied to make an important but provisional point, that axis now withdraws the ontic, value distinctions that once it metered. *Sub species aeternitatis* phenomena are themselves noumena; samsara, nirvana.

> The perfect way knows no difficulties
> Only it refuses to make distinctions.
> A hair's breadth's difference
> And heaven and hell are set apart.
>
> *Seng-ts'an*

Centered in the mathematical point, a non-ego is immune to space and can be where it wishes. "Let us but transport ourselves in spirit outside this world of dimensions and localizations, and there will no longer be need to seek the abode of the Tao," Chuang Tzu tells us (XXII). Transport accomplished, the sage, even while in the flux of things, is at the crux of things. Established in its Unwobbling Pivot, his way of being in the world is *wu wei*. Literally "nonaction," the word does not require that actions cease. Superfluous and ego-aggrandizing activity must be stilled, but the stilling of such activity clears the way for pure effectiveness—action that is powered by force that is concentrated and energy assembled. Far from rendering it ineffectual, the tendency of this second kind of action to "fit in" and avoid calling attention to itself augments its power. "By his simplicity, the absolutely simple man sways all beings. . . . Nothing opposes him in the six regions of space, nothing is hostile to him, and fire and water do not harm him" (*Tao Te Ching*, II). Nothing that comes out of the spaceless point can touch the person who is centered within it.[5] Opposing nothing, nothing can oppose him, for opposition is a reciprocal relationship that requires two terms, which is precisely what unity disallows. Hostility, which is but a consequence or outward manifestation of opposition, can neither proceed from nor be directed toward a being who is beyond all opposition. "Fire and water" in the passage cited stand for the contraries of the phenomenal world; they cannot harm the Simple Man because for him, as contraries, they no longer exist. Neutralizing each other through the union of their seemingly opposed but actually complementing attributes, they have reentered the undifferentiation of the primordial ether. Thus the viewpoint of the Simple Man

is one at which this and that, yes and no, appear still in a state of non-distinction. This point is the Pivot of the Law; it is the motionless center of a circumference on the rim of which all con-

5. "When men shall roll up space as if it were a piece of hide, then shall there be an end of human misery" (Svetasvatara Upanishad).

tingencies, distinctions and individualities revolve. From it only Infinity is to be seen, which is neither this nor that, nor yes nor no. To see all in the yet undifferentiated primoridal unity, or from such a distance that all melts into one, this is true intelligence. *Chuang Tzu*

That which Chuang Tzu calls the Pivot, we, following Guénon, have called the mathematical point. T. S. Eliot celebrated it in lines that have become familiar:

> At the still point of the turning world. Neither flesh nor fleshless;
> Neither from nor towards; at the still point, there the dance is,
> But neither arrest nor movement. And do not call it fixity,
> Where past and future are gathered. Neither movement from
>   nor towards,
> Neither ascent nor decline. Except for the point, the still point,
> There would be no dance, and there is only the dance.[6]

But for the way the cross as a whole, not just its center, can vibrate, our mind goes to Pascal. Mathematician, scientist, philosopher, inventor, whose prose is one of the great glories of France, he could find only incoherent words to describe the disclosure that came to him one memorable night:

> In the year of grace 1654, Monday 23 November, the day of St. Clement, Pope and Martyr, and others in the Martyrology; the eve of St. Chrysostomous, Martyr, and others; from about half-past ten in the evening till about half an hour after midnight

FIRE

> God of Abraham, God of Isaac, God of Jacob. Not of the philosophers and the learned. Certitude. Certitude. Emotion. Joy . . . Joy! Joy! Joy! Tears of Joy . . . My God . . . let me not be separated from thee for ever.

Above this record of his experience, which he kept always on his person, was a rough drawing of a blazing cross. Two-dimensional, but for a Christian, planted unambiguously in Western Europe, it sufficed.

6. "Four Quartets: Burnt Norton," *The Complete Poems and Plays, 1909–1950* (New York: Harcourt, Brace & World, 1952), p. 119.

> Nor was it above my mind as oil above the
> water it floats on, nor as the sky is above earth;
> it was above because it made me, and I was below
> because made by it.
>
> AUGUSTINE, *Confessions*, VII, 10

3. The Levels of Reality

In the opening chapter of this book we argued that the triumphs of modern science went to man's head in something of the way rum does, causing him to grow loose in his logic. He came to think that what science discovers somehow casts doubt on things it does not discover; that the success it realizes in its own domain throws into question the reality of domains its devices cannot touch. In short, he came to assume that science implies scientism: the belief that no realities save ones that conform to the matrices science works with—space, time, matter/energy, and in the end number—exist.

It was not always so, but today a sadness comes over us as we think back over the way this *reductio* leveled the world view that preceded it. Traditionally men had honored, even venerated, their ancestors as being essentially wiser than themselves because closer to the source of things. Now forefathers came to be regarded as "children of the race," laboring under children's immaturity. Their *ens perfectissimum* was a mirage, a wish-fulfilling security blanket spun of thin air to compensate for the hardships of real life. Or alternatively, their convictions regarding the human soul were opiates invented by the privileged to quiet, as if by lobotomy, those who without them might press for a fair share of the world's perquisites.

Reviewing the way the new evicted the old—myopia parading as vision, eternity-blindness as enlightenment and the dawn of a brighter day—we find our thoughts turning to the

Native Americans. They too watched a landscape dismantled, in their case a physical landscape of almost magical richness. Untapped, unravaged, its grains of soil had been to them beads in the garment of the Great Spirit; its trees were temple pillars, its earth too sacred to be trodden save by soft skin moccasins. Across this unparalleled expanse of virgin nature there poured hordes possessing a capacity so strange that they seemed to the natives they dispossessed to represent a different breed:[1] the capacity to look on everything in creation as material for exploitation, seeing trees only as timber, deer only as meat, mountains as no more than potential quarries. For the victims of this "civilizing mission," as the predators chose to call their conquest, there could only be, in the words of a former U.S. Commissioner of Indian Affairs, a "sadness deeper than imagination can hold—sadness of men completely conscious, watching the universe being destroyed by a numberless and scorning foe." For the Indians "had what the world has lost . . . the ancient, lost reverence and passion for human personality joined with the ancient, lost reverence and passion for the earth and its web of life."[2]

Collier's account emphasizes the quality of sadness rather than anger in the Indians' response. Inasmuch as humanity is in some way one, the response may have included an element of pity for us all. In any case, it appears of a piece with our wistfulness as we think of the destruction of the primordial world view that occurred concurrently and relatedly through scientism's reduction of its qualitative aspects to modalities that are basically quantitative. This ontological strip mining asked man to sacrifice a good part of that which made for him

1. Confronted with the novel spectacle of a gorilla in an itinerant circus, a Minnesota medicine man, after subjecting himself to an all-night vigil in a sweat lodge, delivered himself of his judgment. "That," he said, "is a cross between a white man and a cat." Related to the author by a French student of the Ojibways, Jean-Louis Michon.

2. John Collier, *Indians of the Americas* (New York: Mentor Books, 1947), pp. 104, 7; quoted in Gai Eaton, "Man as Viceroy," *Studies in Comparative Religion*, Autumn 1973. We are indebted to the latter article for a number of thoughts on the present subject.

the reality of the world—its beauty, its holiness and crucial expanses of truth—in return for a mathematical scheme whose prime advantage was to help man manipulate matter on its own plane. The discontinuous character of number ordained in advance that such a predominantly quantitative approach would miss the immense tissue of being, its side that consists of pure continuity and relations kept necessarily in balance.

In point of fact, however, continuity and equilibrium exist before discontinuity and crisis; they are more real than these latter and incomparably more precious. But this the modern mind has forgotten. In the face of its lapse, logic can do no more. Short of a historical breakdown which would render routine ineffectual and force us to attend again to things that matter most, we wait for art; for metaphysicians who, imbued with that species of truth that is beauty in its mental mode, are (like Plato) concomitantly poets. By irradiating the human imagination that has atrophied in this *kali yuga*, this age of iron, such men might restore to it the supple, winged condition it requires if it is to come within light-years of Truth. They might return to our inner eye—almost, one might say, to our sense of touch—ontological spaces we have forgotten exist, landscapes crowded with presences the knowing of which can turn men into saints.[3] If the "remembrance of things past" they conjured were vivid enough for us to enter it as confidently as we step out of our front doors, we might, as we have said, rejoin the human race. For to reverse an earlier image, epistemologically their work would be archaeological: a stripping back of deposits of scientistic pseudoinferences that hide the contours, extravagant but defined, of the primordial outlook whose regions appear largely as blanks in the cosmologies modernity has reduced to cosmography.

3. Though few in number, such metaphysicians already exist. For our part, we have found them concentrated among the contributors to a small but luminous journal, *Studies in Comparative Religion* (Pates Manor, Bedford, Middlesex, England). Jacob Needleman has collected selected essays from this journal into a book titled *The Sword of Gnosis* (Baltimore: Penguin Books, 1974).

Archaeology is an appropriate metaphor for the inward probe toward reality, and this we shall come to in the next chapter. For the present, however, we shall table our natural interest in how the levels appear in man and establish their existence in their own right. This calls for reverting to outbound, stratospheric imagery, a mounting of the vertical arm of the three-dimensional cross as it pierces through "cloudlands"—in the last resort they are all maya—to the apex that alone is fully real, the Infinite.

Disregarding domains that are inferior to our own and therefore lie below the horizontal arm of the cross, common numbering of the worlds is threefold: terrestrial, intermediary, and celestial. Beyond these three lies a fourth domain that is discontinuous with the others. Not itself a world, it is the Infinite which is their uncreated source.

1. The Terrestrial Plane

We begin with the terrestrial plane, which alternatively we shall call the gross, the material, the sensible, the corporeal, the phenomenal, or the human plane. Strictly speaking, the last of these appellations is a misnomer, because, as we have mentioned in passing already and will consider in detail in the next chapter, man in the fullness of his being intersects the planes in their entirety. Even so, the designation is convenient, for the plane in question is the one we are most directly in touch with. Its distinctive categories are space, time, energy/matter, and number, the last being a mode to which the first three lend themselves.

Four is a schematization, of course, for the actual number is (as we have said) indefinite. And because the four are in reality classes, we can expect subdivisions to appear in each. These are most apparent on the terrestrial plane, where animal, vegetable, and mineral demarcate themselves obviously; the other planes are difficult enough to see in overview without trying to read the fine print. On the terrestrial plane an upper, border region announces itself in the data that frontier physics encounters. Such data belong to the terrestrial world inasmuch as they continue to participate in some way in space, time, and matter/energy as quantifiable, but the way in which they so participate is, to say the least, peculiar. In this twilight border region, parallel lines converge, things relocate without traversing space, and particles have only probable positions. Phenomena are beginning to phase out of the grossly physical. The terrestrial announces its dependence on the plane above it.

2. The Intermediate Plane

This next plane up is named, neutrally, the intermediate.[4] Alternatively we shall refer to it as the subtle, the animic,[5] or the psychic plane, inasmuch as it is often encountered in phantasms that have no sensible counterparts.

These phantasms can be animate or inanimate: the plane houses both. Those that are animate are the various species of

4. The term goes back to Plato's *to metaxy*, a view which Paul Friedländer says "must have been of the utmost significance to him. It is the idea or view of 'the demonic' as a realm 'intermediate' between the human level and the divine, a realm that because of its intermediate position 'unites the cosmos with itself.' " *Plato*, Vol. I *An Introduction* (London: Routledge & Kegan Paul, 1958), p. 41; see *Republic*, X614c. Thomas Aquinas's general formulation of the point is as follows: "Ordo rerum talis esse invenitur, ut ab uno extremo ad alterum non perveniatur nisi per media"; the order of reality is found to be such that it is impossible to reach one end from the other without passing through the middle.

For a global depiction of this level of existence, see Edward Conze, "The Intermediary World," *The Eastern Buddhist*, VI, 2 (Oct. 1974). Beginning with the statement that "the spiritual tradition of mankind has everywhere and at all times taught that there is a *triple* world, the natural world, the spiritual world, and a world intermediary between the two" (p. 23), Conze proceeds to focus on this middle sphere as it appears in his special field of scholarship, Buddhism. "A belief in the existence of an intermediary world is attested in all Buddhist scriptures a thousand times. No Buddhist community has ever been without it. It is also, incidentally, reflected in the trikaya doctrine [of the] three ways of looking at a Buddha" (p. 24).

5. We are forced to this neologism because the word "animistic" has come to be identified with a doctrine.

discarnates: ghosts; departed souls that are provisionally in limbo, or traversing the intermediate *bardos* (planes), as the Tibetans would say; the "controls" that spiritualists and mediums claim to be in touch with insofar as their claims are valid; and our own subtle bodies (*suksma-sarira*) insofar as they are disengaged, as in sleep, from their gross, exterior envelopes. These subtle bodies are often called "etheric" or "astral," and their adventures—central to shamanism—described as astral projections, but we must remember that spatial imagery never fits precisely on planes above our own. The highest planes contain no literal space whatever. The intermediate plane is spatial in a way, but the way differs markedly from that of terrestrial space: the peculiarities that we just noted in post-Newtonian physics derive from the fact that its novelties are first steps in the direction of space of the intermediary order. All this must be kept in mind when we hear talk of astral projection and the dream journeys of shamans. As with everything on the higher planes, such notions become absurd if we force them into terrestrial armor, a costuming that in this case generates pictures of psychic pellets slipping through dermal pores to rocket this way or that to who knows what fantastic wonderlands. The truth at issue will emerge if we balance such astronautical images with opposing ones in which the subtle body remains securely within its corporeal sheath while time and space wash through it, and its indriyic net—*indriyas*: subtle correlates of our physical sense organs (Sanskrit)—selects the information it seeks. Or let the explanatory model be ESP, the psychic counterpart of gravitation's action at a distance. This eliminates spatial imagery altogether.

Passing to the impersonal furniture of the psychic plane, we encounter most importantly the archetypes.[6] Their actual

6. The word compounds notions of (a) antiquity, as in "archaeololgy," and by extension timelessness or primordiality; (b) superlative rank or status, as in "archduke" and "archbishop"; and (c) norm or exemplar, from the Greek *arketupon*, meaning "that which was created as a pattern, mold, or model."

abode is on the next plane up, but lower planes derive from the higher, so the archetypes appear on the subtle plane as reflections of their originals—each world in creation is no more than a tissue of shadows entirely dependent on the archetypes in the world above, phenomena being (as we might say) divine qualities eroded in an illusory manner by nothingness. Thus the archetypes turn up on the terrestrial plane as well, in the "forms" that shape objects out of a matter that would otherwise be inchoate.[7] On the subtle plane which we are currently considering, however, we encounter them more directly, though not yet unalloyed.

When on the next plane we do find them in their unalloyed state, they turn out to be Plato's Forms or Ideas, but here on the intermediate plane they stand closer to the archetypes Jung explored. The images he found recurring in the dreams of his patients coincided to such a degree with the world's mythologies (of which his patients were largely innocent) that he concluded that the symbols themselves must reside in man's collective unconscious. But not passively—not as colors on a painter's palette, to be dipped into for the artist's needs. They have an energy of their own, sufficient to have caused Jung to regard them as the psychic counterparts of biological instincts. Physically man's life is vectored by his biological drives; psychically it is molded by the surging pressure of the archetypes. In the end Jung risked a further correlation. The archetypes seemed close enough to the patterns he saw emerging in the theories and experiments of twentieth-century physics for him to conclude that archetypes are *psychoid*. By this he meant that they shape matter (nature) as well as mind (psyche). They transcend the split between these two and are neutral toward it, favoring neither one side nor the other.[8]

7. If one must try for metaphors, archetypes may be likened to invisible magnetic fields which iron filings visibly conform to. Archetypes prescribe the *kind* of experience we shall have, but *what* we experience is individual.

8. If Jung had seen this early in his career and based his psychology squarely upon it, his thought could have been in line with the primordial

This account has a double virtue. First, it establishes the fact that the intermediate plane governs the terrestrial plane in its entirety, its corporeal as well as its psychic aspects; to underscore the completeness of its suzerainty, Sufis call it the Domain of Royalty (*malakut*). The Indian notion of siddhis— yogic powers, certain of which can influence external bodies directly, in psychokinesis as we would say—moves in the same direction, as does the concept of magic as the action of subtle force on corporeal matter.

The second respect in which Jung's notion of archetypes is appropriate here is in the justice it does to their formative powers; they "create" or project forth the terrestrial plane, which is no more than their exterior covering. Several times in this study we have inveighed against reductionism, but let us be clear. Its error does not lie in its attempt to understand one type of reality in terms of another. Virtually all explanation proceeds in this fashion, and explanation is needed, for true reality is never the most obvious; one might almost say that one of the ways truth betrays the fact that it is such is in the care it takes to remain elusive, if one may put the matter paradoxically. The mistake of reductionism—spirit reduced to metamorphosed matter (Darwinism), truth reduced to ideology (Marxism), psyche reduced to sex (Freud: there is no way "to sweeten the sour apple")—lies in its attempt to explain the greater in terms of the less, with the not surprising consequence that the greater is thereby lessened. It is this, at root, that sets us against the modern outlook and turns us back toward tradition where the drift is always the reverse: to

tradition. As it was, his psychoid thesis was an addendum—one, moreover, that his followers have resisted, preferring on the whole his standard contention that archetypes derive from the collective unconscious that has evolved in the course of human evolution. This, Jung's prevailing contention, was part and parcel of his lifelong struggle to have his theories accepted as scientific, a struggle that produced not only inconsistencies in his "system," but his own version of psychological reductionism; see Titus Burckhardt, "Cosmology and Modern Science," in Needleman, *The Sword of Gnosis*, pp. 153–78. In quoting Jung approvingly, we must be selective.

explain the lesser by means of the more, a mode of explanation that tends to augment rather than deplete, for in both cases explanation produces a kind of rub-off. The terrestrial plane proceeds from and is explained by the intermediate, the intermediate by the celestial, and the celestial by the Infinite. Thus everything derives, ultimately, from the Infinite. And since "derives" cannot in this last case involve separation—the Infinite is like a celestial void: nothing escapes from it—everything abides in the Infinite's luster.[9]

We tend to think of mind as an epiphenomenon, as a gloss on matter with spirit a patina on that gloss. The truth is the reverse. Matter is the rarity; it obtrudes from the psychic with perhaps the frequency of a few stalactites from the roof of an enormous cavern. Or it is like our earth and its planets—tiny bits of matter floating in an ocean of space. Our lives are plunged in the animic world like crystals floating in a liquid, though appearances make us suppose that the animic is within our bodies or behind the physical shell of things. This supposition causes us to underrate the mental. Apart from the fact that it closes the door on the domain to which magic pertains, it again makes the higher depend on the lower and keeps us from seeing the faculties that make man distinctively human in their full extent.

This holds not only when these faculties are in working order, but when they are not.[10] Insanity is now regarded as "mental illness": we place its victims in hospitals and pity them in the way we do those who have lost their bodily health. (The victims themselves often dispute this assessment, of course, but they are the ones who are mad, so their judgment is

9. "All primordial men . . . saw the 'more' in the 'less,' in the sense that the landscape was for them a reflection of a superior reality which 'contained' the physical reality; they added, may one say, to the latter, a 'spiritual dimension' which escapes modern man." (Francois Petitpierre, "The Symbolic Landscape of the Muiscas," *Studies in Comparative Religion*, Winter 1975, p. 48).

10. On this subject we are again indebted to Gai Eaton's "Man as Viceroy."

discounted.) In point of fact, however, insanity is seldom simply a lack. We recognize this, despite the changes we have effected in vocabulary, in the fear that insanity, unlike disease, continues to inspire within us, the inkling of strange seas beating against the shores of our familiar island. A man may have "lost his reason" only to have had it replaced, for better or worse, by something else. Rarely is he simply reduced like an amputee, and when we treat him as such he feels deeply if obscurely insulted even if we are insensitive to our impertinence.

Mindful of the psychic plane and the way the human is lodged within it, traditional societies tend to regard the insane with a species of awe and respect, seeing them as caught in psychic vortices that work at cross-purposes to ours while possessing something of the autonomy and coherence that ours exhibit. Our madhouses, too, may contain souls that are ravaged by principalities and powers on the psychic plane; in a word, possessed. The phenomenal response to a recent film, *The Exorcist*, shows that our unconscious minds remain open to this notion, but current psychiatric theory is so opposed to it that it will be useful to have an example to show that there are cases that almost require it.[11] The following eyewitness account by Peter Goullart is condensed from his book *The Monastery of Jade Mountain*:[12]

> The energumen, a rather emaciated man of about twenty-five, lay on an iron bedstead on a rush mat. He was very pale and there was a wild, roving look in his fevered eyes. The Taoist priest, holding an elongated ivory tablet held ceremonially in both hands in

11. There is another reason for citing an actual instance: clear cases appear to be less common today than in the past. This may be due in part to the fact that persons tend to be receptive to what they believe— Freudians have a disproportionate number of Freudian dreams—and possession does not square with the modern scientific outlook, but there is a supplementing possibility. With genocides and the use of nuclear weapons to mash entire countrysides, the demonic may now be so diffused on the terrestrial plane that it has no need, one almost says no time, to put in many "personal appearances" in single individuals.

12. London: John Murray, 1961, pp. 86–89.

front of his chest, approached the bed slowly. There was a visible transformation on the energumen's face. His eyes were filled with malice as he watched the priest's measured advance with a sly cunning and hatred. Suddenly he gave a bestial whoop and jumped up in his bed, the four attendants rushing to hold him.

"No! No! You cannot drive us out. We are two against one. Our power is greater than yours." The sentences poured out of the energumen's distorted mouth in a strange, shrill voice, which sounded mechanical, inhuman—as if pronounced by a parrot. The priest looked at the victim intensely, gathering all his inner strength; beads of perspiration appeared on his thin face.

"Come out! Come out! I command you to come out!" He was repeating in a strong metallic voice with great force. "I am using the power of the One compared to whom you are nothing. In His name I command you to come out." Inmobile, he continued to focus his powers on the energumen's face. The man was struggling in the bed with incredible strength against the four men who held him. Animal growls and howls issued from time to time from his mouth which became square, his teeth gleaming like the fangs of a dog. I had the impression that a pack of wild animals was fighting inside his body. Terrible threats poured out of the contorted mouth, now fringed in white foam, and interspersed with such incredible obscenities that women had to plug their ears with their fingers.

Again the abbot cried his command to the unseen adversaries to leave the prostrate man. There was a burst of horrible laughter from the victim's throat and suddenly with a mighty heave of his supernaturally strengthened arms he threw off the men who held him and jumped at the priest's throat like a mad bloodhound. But he was over-powered again. This time they bound him with ropes and fastened the ends to the bedposts. The abbot, still immobile, continued his conjurations in a metallic voice, his eyes never leaving the body. With unutterable horror, we saw that it began to swell visibly. On and on the dreadful process continued until he became a grotesque balloon of a man.

"Leave him! Leave him!" cried the monk concentrating still harder. Convulsion shook the monstrous swollen body. It seemed that all the apertures of the body were opened by the unseen powers hiding in it and streams of malodorous excreta and effluvia flowed on to the ground in incredible profusion. For an hour this continued and then the energumen, resuming his normal size, seemed to come to rest, with his eyes watching the unmoved priest who was still reading.

The priest stopped reading; with sweat pouring down his face, he backed down to the altar, laid down the tablet and took up the ritual sword. Threateningly and commandingly he stood again over the energumen.

"The struggle is useless!" he cried. "Leave him! Leave him in the name of the Supreme Power who never meant you to steal this man's body!" Another scene of horror evolved itself before our dazed eyes. The man on the bed became rigid and his muscles seemed to contract, turning him into a figure of stone. Slowly, very slowly, the iron bedstead, as if impelled by an enormous weight, caved in, its middle touching the ground. The attendants seized the inert man by his feet and arms. The weight was such that none of them could lift him up and they asked for assistance from the onlookers. Seven men could hardly lift him for he was heavy as a cast-iron statue. Suddenly he became light again and they put him on a wooden bed which had been brought in. A long time passed with the abbott reading and commanding interminably. At last he sprinkled the inert man with holy water and advanced to him again with a sword. His concentration was so deep that he did not seem to see anybody. He was utterly exhausted and swayed slightly. Two novices came up to support him.

"I have won!" he cried triumphantly in a strange voice. "Get out! Get out!" The energumen stirred and fell into dreadful convulsions. His eyes rolled up and only the whites were visible. His breathing was stertorous and he clawed his body until he was covered with blood. Foam was issuing from his mouth and a loud gurgling sound.

"Damn you! Damn you!" came a wild scream from the foaming lips. "We are going but you shall pay for it with your life." There was a terrific struggle on the bed, the poor man twisting and rolling like a mortally-wounded snake and his colour changing all the time. Suddenly he fell flat on his back and was still. His eyes opened. His gaze was normal and he saw his parents who now came forward.

"My parents!" he cried weakly. "Where am I" He was very feeble and they carried him out in a specially ordered sedan chair. The abbott himself was in a terrible state of prostration and was half-carried and half-dragged away by his novices.

The word "possession" usually, as here, connotes demonic possession, and this underscores the fact that the psychic plane houses evil as well as good. For the popular mind, which (as we have seen) ranks the worlds on the scale of euphoria, this fact necessitates splitting the psychic plane in two: lodging its beatific components in heavens above the earth and its hellish ones in realms below—the effect can be achieved by rounding the intermediate plane into a circle that envelops the terrestrial plane. But for the reflective mind whose ordering principle is power—and more basically, being—the moral and affective differences that loom so large in popular thought are secondary. Evil is worse than good, but its power

can rival it at points, which means that at these points the two are ontically on a par. And if the power in question exceeds the terrestrial, this par lies above the terrestrial plane.[13] The primordial, Zarathustrian war between the opposites proceeds

13. This variability—between being and euphoria as the unit of measure—explains why certain medieval cosmologists place the hells symbolically between heaven and earth, and why in Islam it is said that the throne of the devil is to be found between earth and heaven.

on the intermediate plane; we inherit its spill and backwash. Sufis recognize the ambiguous character of the psychic plane by calling it God's Footstool—the place where Rigor and Mercy, his two feet, reside—whereas the celestial plane is his Throne: that plane is beatific throughout, for on his throne God sits complete. According to the Tibetan Book of the Dead, the intermediate *bardos* (planes) that a soul must traverse before it reenters a human body run the full gamut from terror to bliss. The opposites they house are the same as those we experience here, but there they are experienced more intensely. We visit those *bardos* nightly, the Indians say, when, subtle bodies disjoined from gross, we dream.

A final point about the intermediate plane brings up again the place of space and time within it. We have already noted that this plane does not elude these categories entirely; for this reason it can be classed with the terrestrial plane, the two together constituting the manifest world or nature in the inclusive meaning of these terms.[14] It can even be the object of empirical research as in parapsychology and depth psychology, though the teeth on the rim of its wheel, so to speak, are rather flexible and barely mesh with the cogs of consensual objectivity which even these sciences, if they are to be such, must honor as the final indices of the real.[15] But though space and

14. The modern restriction of the word "nature" to the terrestrial plane represents a contraction. The Latin *natura* is a translation of the Greek *physis*, which "originally encompassed heaven as well as earth. . . . *Physis* means the power that emerges and the enduring realm under its sway." Martin Heidegger, *An Introduction to Metaphysics* (Garden City, N.Y.: Doubleday and Co., 1961), p. 12.

15. Isolated instances of psi phenomena, however dramatic, will never convince everyone, for the same reasons that there will never be a knock-down proof of a miracle. As for statistics—whether on average the mind, or certain minds, can exceed the laws of chance in predicting falls of dice or runs of cards—the situation will remain where it has stood since such investigations began. The results exceed probability, but so marginally (to say nothing of the fact that the probabilities are violated negatively as well as positively) that, given legitimate differences of interpretation in the logical foundations of statistics themselves, it remains reasonable to believe or disbelieve in the powers in question. No more here than anywhere can the lower prove the existence of the higher on the former's

time pertain in some ways to the psychic realm, the ways themselves are significantly different from those that hold on the gross, corporeal plane. To accommodate the psychic counterparts of the spatio-temporal peculiarities that manifest themselves in frontier physics, Jung coined the word "synchronicity." We need not juggle the full theory behind that word; our interest is in a single point. If Jung was accurate in reporting that meaningful "coincidences"—as in Arthur Koestler's *The Roots of Coincidence*—increased for his patients as they became aware of the archetypal symbols and situations that were working in their lives, this fact supports our present thrust. In addition to creating the terrestrial world, the archetypes order it in ways that partially exceed its linear laws of causation.

3. The Celestial Plane

The intermediate plane is not a miscellany. It is not even enough to say that it is an integrated and ordered whole. One must add that it is a conscious whole, for as one mounts the levels of being, awareness intensifies and integration increases. The subtle state coalesces in its totality in the "universal or total soul," as Plotinus called it, though in the terminology we are using it is the universal or total mind. As with organs and the organisms of which they are members, individual minds can be distinguished from the world mind, but they are not separate from it.

The world mind is the supreme expression of the divine in the manifest world, but it is far from God's totality. The ques-

---

terms, however much on other terms, by other sensibilities, it all but bursts with transcendent cargo. The opinion of one of the most respected current researchers in parapsychology, 1974–75 president of the Association for Humanistic Psychology, is, on this point, worth quoting. After noting that a recent poll of the largely professional readership of the British journal *The New Scientist* found only 3 percent to believe that paranormal phenomena are impossible, Stanley Krippner adds: Nevertheless,"psychic phenomena are so fragile and so unpredictable that I believe that they are beyond complete control." *Psychology Today*, Oct. 1973, p. 110.

tion of what more his nature contains carries us to the plane above the intermediate, the celestial.

When a man effects a project—wages a campaign, let us say —he is truly present within it. A part of his nature surfaces in the campaign, clearer than if we had been left to infer how he might have performed in the face of its demands. Even so, the undertaking treats us to but a facet of his being. We assume that underlying *what* the person does is the person who does those things. In the case in question, he involves himself in the campaign, but by no stretch of the imagination can he be equated with this involvement.

Comparably with God. To the end that nothing that is possible be left undone—if it were, the Infinite would not be such—God actualizes (creates) being in the mode of mutiplicity and individuation. In addition he enters and abides in his creation—the terrestrial and intermediate planes combined—as the mind that organizes and empowers it. All the while he transcends his creation and exceeds his involvement with it. According to Hindu cosmology, during the nights of Brahma in which he sleeps, the terrestrial and intermediate planes vanish completely; the "big bang" reverses—matter vanishes into spreading black holes?—leaving nothing for the (no longer existing) astronomers to detect. The lower realms, now reabsorbed into the celestial, are shown to have been but episodes in the divine expanse.[16]

Mystics, endowed with the "eye of the heart," can intuit this celestial expanse; others must rely on reports or inferences. Regarding the last of these, we have noted more than once that unaided logic can infer nothing regarding higher realms from ones that have been severed from them completely—realms viewed only in terms of what excludes them from ones that are higher: the externality of their components, their fragmentari-

16. "Our world is but a furtive and almost accidental coagulation of an immense 'beyond,' which one day will burst forth and in which the terrestrial world will be reabsorbed when it has completed its cycle of material coagulation." Frithjof Schuon, *Logic and Transcendence* (New York: Harper & Row, 1975), p. 94.

ness, their incorrigible limitations. But if a lower plane is viewed through the eyes of what might be called "ontic sensibility,"[17] it is noticed that the plane is illumined. Seeking the source of its illumination, sight turns upward and logic perceives the contours of the planes from which the illumination issues.

Such "ontological logic" points invariably toward greater being and less division. Thus the celestial plane dwarfs the ones below it in the plenitude of its existence and at the same time is less fragmented. Multiplicity reduces in its case to the basic *kinds* of existents, the archetypes; we encountered them in a derivative mode on the intermediate plane, but come now upon the originals which, combining and recombining, give form and structure to the worlds below.

To us these "universals," as they are sometimes called, seem abstract, for in the phenomenal world we never encounter beauty, say, by itself but only as a property of concrete things that are beautiful. However, to regard objects as concrete and their properties abstract is like calling water spray concrete and wetness abstract. Objects are ephemeral, qualities endure; the qualities we encounter in tangible objects are fragile attenuations of the intense, undiluted, and stable condition the archetypes enjoy in their own right, on their own plane. In addition to archetypes of single qualities, there are archetypes that are combinations of these. A species is an instance. Roses come from Roseness, which is incomparably more real than the flowers that line the garden walk.

The celestial plane can be viewed impersonally, in which case the archetypes are, as we noted earlier by way of anticipa-

17. The intuitive discernment that (a) nothing can arise without a cause, (b) causes are greater than their effects, (c) the greater is more integrated, and (d) the sequence of greaters cannot stop short of the Greatest, the Infinite. "The role of the sage is not—as in the radically mistaken view of Europeans—to explain things from zero and to construct a system, but firstly to 'see' and secondly to 'cause to see,' that is, to provide a key." Frithjof Schuon, *Islam and the Perennial Philosophy* (London: World of Islam Festival Publishing Company Ltd, 1976), p. 149.

tion, the Platonic forms; viewed collectively, as comprising and implying one another, they constitute the Idea of the Good. It is more natural, however, to use personal imagery, for of things we directly know, persons are the best, and as we ascend the ladder of reality, value keeps step with being. Even Plato uses personal terms when in the *Sophist* he has the Eleatic stranger attribute to the "friends of the forms" the view that the forms are alive. Plotinus in typical fashion converts Plato's allusion into settled fact: the forms are unequivocally alive, which makes the Intelligence that comprehends them even more so. In conventional terminology the celestial plane is the abode of God Transcendent: God before he creates the world and the fullness of God that exceeds his creation after he has accomplished it. It goes without saying that God's nature is integrated, but this does not keep it from being composed of attributes. It is meaningful to speak of his love, his will, his judgment, his mercy, and the like.[18]

We are obviously here in the realm of theism in its classic Western sense. The celestial sphere is the sphere of the personal God. God of Abraham, Isaac, and Jacob rather than of the philosophers, he creates the world by deliberate intent, presides over history providentially, and knows and loves his creatures —not a sparrow falls but he registers that fact (Matt. 10:29); "not so much as the weight of an ant in heaven and earth escapes from Him" (Koran, XXXIV:3).

About theism in this eminently personal mode three points must be made:

1. The view is natural. Satirists, eyes peeled for man's pretensions, use this as a count against it: "If cattle . . . were able

18. Cosmologies frequently locate the archetypes and God on separate ontological planes with God as the higher of the two. When this separation is effected the principal levels of reality number five instead of the four we are employing. Though the archetypes can be regarded as God's first creations, to keep the paradigm this book presents to simplest possible proportions we are regarding them as his attributes, in the way Plotinus identified Intelligence (*Nous*) with its objects (the Platonic forms) and Augustine saw these forms as God's "divine ideas."

to draw . . . they would make the bodies of the gods such as they had themselves," said Xenophanes; the gods of triangles, said Montesquieu, would have three sides. But there is no reason to disparage what is natural; as a rule it tokens what is fit and appropriate. To be put off by the anthropomorphic character of God in scripture amounts in last resort to being disaffected with ourselves, for the reality we call God necessarily assumes toward us a human demeanor to the end that we may enter as fully as possible into what is ultimately impenetrable. "Thought flows into man," said Shankara, "as molten metal is poured into the founder's mold." The very intensity of the God-idea makes it occupy man wholly, more or less as water fills a vessel to the brim. It assumes the shape of that which contains and limits it, and becomes anthropomorphic.

But is God personal only in the way he appears to us, or is he personal in himself, in his own right and nature? This introduces the second point.

2. Theism is true. It is not the final truth; God's personal mode is not his final mode; it is not the final reality. Even so, it is vastly more real than are the creatures who encounter him in this mode, so the fact that the mode is not final presents no problem. Only persons who sense *themselves* to be not finally real—*anatta*, no-self—will sense the same of the God of theism. And for them it does not matter that in the last analysis God is not the kind of God who loves them, for at this level there is no "them" to be loved. Insofar as one takes oneself seriously, as all of us do most of the time and most of us do all of the time, the God of theism is to be taken seriously too. Not only do we love; we are loved. Not only do we hope; we are hoped for. Not only do we find or miss meaning; we are meant.

Nevertheless:

3. Theism is not the final truth. Its vision of God is modeled after capacities that are distinctively human, and noble as these capacities are—the capacity to make discriminating judgments, the capacity to exercise responsible decision and choice, the ability to carry out long-range purposes—they require for

their exercise contexts that stand over and against their subject and thereby limit him. But the final reality is unlimited, for it is infinite; to put the point in an aphorism, nothing *finite* can be *final*.[19] Being persons ourselves, we tend to see in God the part or aspect of his nature that is kin to us. But part is never whole: man *has* reflexes (knee jerks, eye blinks); he is not *himself* a reflex, not in his wholeness. Or to move closer to the dignity of the topic at hand, man possesses reason while at the same time exceeding his possession: reason is his tool, not his definition. Several paragraphs above we noted that God is anthropomorphic. Now we add that there is a sense in which he is not; to wit, the sense in which he transcends all descriptions, anthropomorphic ones included—mystics often use the word "Godhead" for this transpersonal mode. Religious sensibility demands this correlate as much as does logic, for much as we yearn for a God who resembles us, such a God could never satisfy us completely: we know ourselves too well.[20] It is a truism that a God we could comprehend would not command our worship. If he could be squeezed into the miserably inadequate vessel of our minds we would not avert our eyes—no shudder would run through us; there would be no *horror religiosus*, no religious awe. It is not enough to say that God's attributes exceed ours inexhaustibly; the attributes themselves must be transcended, for in the last analysis they derive, all but infinity, from limitation, which finally is what religion works to transcend.[21] The difference in degree must phase into a difference in kind.

19. "There is one logically inescapable conception, and it is that of infinity, of that which has no limit of any kind. It is impossible to conceive of an absolute limit; for it would have to be as it were a one-sided boundary, a door having an inside face but no outside face." Lord Northbourne, *Religion in the Modern World* (London: Perennial Books, 1970), p. 30.

20. "If He is like us, we are lost," Ignatius of Antioch wrote to the Magnesians on his way to Rome for his martyrdom. I am indebted to Father Martin Boler of Mount Savior Monastery, Pine City, New York, for this reference.

21. "Great art suggests . . . ideal forms . . . in terms of . . . appearances; but what is art to one that toils up the Unshown Way, seeking to

4. The Infinite

"The difference between most people and myself," wrote Jung toward the close of his life, "is that for me the 'dividing walls' are transparent."[22] Remove the walls entirely, including any that might serve as boundaries or perimeters, and we have God in his ultimate nature: the Infinite.

As with God in his personal mode, so too with his Infinite. Several points must be registered, in this case four.

1. Only negative terms characterize it literally.[23] This begins with the word "Infinite" itself, which asserts only that its object is not finite, and holds equally for other characterizations such as unconditioned, ineffable, and immutable. In Hinduism

---

transcend all limitations of the human intellect, to reach a plane of being unconditioned even by ideal form? For such an one, the most refined and intellectual delights are but flowery meadows where men may linger and delay, while the straight path to utter truth waits vainly for the traveller's feet. The thought explains the belief that absolute emancipation is hardly won by any but human beings yet incarnate; it is harder for the Gods to attain such release, for their pure and exalted bliss and knowledge are attachments even stronger than those of earth." Ananda K. Coomaraswamy, "The Aims of Indian Art," *Studies in Comparative Religion*, Winter 1975, p. 9.

22. C. G. Jung, *Memories, Dreams, Reflections* (New York: Vintage Books, 1961), p. 355.

23. "Sacred Writers . . . call It Nameless [because it] is fixed beyond every name that is named, not only in this world but also in that which is to come." Dionysius the Areopagite, *The Divine Names and The Mystical Theology*, trans. by C. E. Rolt (London: S.P.C.K., 1971), p. 61. Here Dionysius's accent is on the fact that the Godhead can not be named, but elsewhere he adds that it should not be named. For two thousand years Jews have been forbidden to pronounce the tetragrammaton YHVH, and its vocalization is no longer known. Islam lists ninety-nine names of Allah; the hundredth is silent. All this is in keeping with an Akka pygmy chief's declaration that "God is He whose Name must not even be pronounced."

We make a point of including the pygmy's assertion to build into this book a conviction which, because we have not ourselves worked directly with tribal religions, is little documented in these pages and is left to ride almost wholly on the allusion to Mircea Eliade's work on page 3; namely, the conviction that the primordial tradition covers not only the great historical traditions but archaic ones as well. With respect to Native American traditions, Joseph Epes Brown's accounts in particular seem to support this conviction.

the Infinite is *nir*-guna (without qualities); in Buddhism it is *nir*-vana (nondrawing, as a fire whose fuel is exhausted has ceased to draw) and sunyata (emptiness, a void); in Taoism it is the Tao that cannot be spoken; in Judaism it is *'en-sof*, the not-finite. The Infinite cannot be defined positively because definitions compare: either they liken what they define to something or they distinguish it from something. If they distinguish, we are back with negation: the object defined is not what it is contrasted with. And if they liken? But the Infinite is all-inclusive, so there is nothing other than it to which it *can* be likened.

2. Positive terms apply to the Infinite only analogically. When Vedantists say that Brahman is *Sat*, *Chit*, and *Ananda* (Being, Awareness, and Bliss) they mean that the terms are more accurate than their opposites. The Infinite is more like a lion that exists than like a unicorn that does not, more like creatures that experience than like objects that do not, more like ourselves when we are fulfilled than when we are wanting. But that is all the assertions claim. We cannot presume that Being in its infinity bears more than a trace of resemblance to the being we encounter in rocks or mountains or waterfalls. And because the connotation of "being" derives preponderantly from the modes in which we encounter it directly, it would be misleading to claim that the word characterizes the Infinite literally. Only if the claim is converted into its negation—the assertion that the Infinite hasn't zero-being (doesn't not-exist) —is it literally true; short of this the word functions analogically. The same holds for "awareness," "bliss," and all other posited attributes.

3. The degree to which positive terms seem apposite will vary. The reason is: it depends on the experience (or the imaginative capacity) of the person who is using them. When Spinoza said that God's knowledge resembles our knowledge to the extent that the Dog Star resembles a dog, it was because in his discernment the Infinite exceeded the finite in about that ratio. Others whose "ceilings" are lower will not find the disparity as

great. The governing law reads: the more developed the sense of the Infinite, the more distant from the finite it appears and the less literal positive designations will seem.

4. The most effective way to underscore the negative side of analogy—how much attributes when predicated of the Infinite differ from the modes in which we usually encounter them—is through paradox. The device can also be seen as one by which the mystics who (to borrow one of their own profound words) have "suffered" the weight of the Infinite try to raise the sensibility ceilings of the uninitiated with respect to the Infinite's otherness. The opposing forces that paradox generates cause it to function as a verbal lever. The mystic may begin, for example, by establishing as fulcrum the fact that God is light. This holds both metaphorically (light everywhere symbolizes knowledge) and literally inasmuch as God-incursion is often accompanied by light that is physically sensed: Christ in his transfiguration, Saul on the Damascus road, saints in the Eastern Orthodox tradition. But in saying "light" the mystic will be misunderstood, for neither the literal nor the symbolic light he intends is the light the world knows—on the literal side, for example, it has the power of an arc lamp with no sense of glare or strain. Immediately, therefore, he must press against the word's usual connotations. So: "God is not light"; if "light" denotes its conventional referents, God is darkness. The countervailing forces raise the far end of the lever toward light of a different order. If the alchemy works, our minds are expanded and our souls as well.[24]

24. The following paraphrase of a commentary by Martin Lings on the aphorisms of the Shaikh Ahmad al-Alawi further amplifies the dynamics of this exceptional mode of discourse: Since wisdom is in fact a hidden treasure, it is not always uneloquent to present it as such. In the case of paradox, however, an additional element is involved. The barbed shaft of the unexpected is introduced to penetrate the hearer and goad him into a state of spiritual vigilance, keying his understanding to a higher pitch. Here too the expression corresponds to an aspect of what is expressed, for the truth is in fact strange, and the mind should not be allowed the complacency of supposing that it is familiar with more than a fragment of it, seen from a particular angle. *A Sufi Saint of the Twentieth Century* (Berkeley: University of California Press, 1971), p. 204.

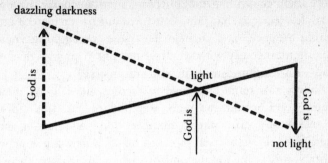

These four points speak to language and the Infinite. What within their stipulations need be added before this chapter may close?

Of the (necessarily negative) predicates that apply to the Infinite literally, the most important two are "unbounded" and "undifferentiated"—we are back with the fact that walls, internal *or* peripheral, dividing *or* enclosing, have no place at being's summit. The Infinite is unbounded because as we have had more than one occasion to remark, a boundary would limit it and contradict its infinity. It is undifferentiated,[25] because differentiation implies distinction and thereby in some respect separation, separation in turn implies distance, and in the realm of the spirit distance symbolizes ignorance epistemologically and privation affectively. A Something that excludes nothing save distinctions we cannot begin to image[26] any

25. "He goes from death to death who sees anything like manyness here." Katha Upanishad, II.i.10.

26. If in the face of this fact the mind persists in erecting images, one type in particular must be warned against: namely, the kind that pictures nondifferentiation as a blank: a cloudless sky, a sea uncloven by waves, a field of unbroken light. Such images err because they conspicuously, almost self-consciously, exclude. They obviously exclude clouds and waves and shapes-and-hues of any form, but more seriously (and contrary to their intent) they exclude timelessness. For all of the foregoing images are static, and "static"—implying as it does a something that fails to change with time—is a temporal concept. An instant is not static; therefore, to invoke images that are static betrays the fact that temporal matrices have not yet been transcended. If we cannot resist trying to

more than we can image light that is simultaneously wave and particle, electrons that jump orbit without traversing the intervening distance, or a particle that passes through alternative slits simultaneously without dividing. But if physics does not stop with the image-able, need metaphysics?

Physics can relinquish imagery because it still has mathematics' terra firma to walk on. Metaphysics lacks this support. It reaches a point where, numbers long ago having been abandoned, thought itself faces a drop-off. There are some who mistake this point for the end of the world; whatever can be neither imaged nor coherently conceived, they argue, does not exist. But truth does not need us and is in no way dependent upon our powers of conceptualization. There are regions of being—the unimaginable perfection of totality is at the moment the case in point—that are quite unrelated to the contours of the human mind. The mind is comfortable with facts and fictions.[27] It is not made for grasping ultimates.

Other persons concede that the fact that we cannot conceive of something is no proof that it does not exist, but contend that if it does exist it is for all practical purposes irrelevant.[28] But

---

imagine what the Infinite is like, we will do better to replace lifeless images like the ones just cited with recollections of times when we were so completely engrossed in what we were doing that ingredient components did not present themselves as such and we lost track of time entirely, whether as stoppd or as continuing. Mystics return repeatedly to the climax of sexual love as the most natural human approximation. It is to offset simplistic readings of "simple" as a metaphysical predicate that Advaitic (a = non, dva = dual) Vedantists say, "Never say 'one'; say 'not-two.'" Another way to make the point is to say that "the One . . . is the transcendence of separability rather than the negation of plurality." Quoted in The Essential Plotinus, trans. by Elmer O'Brien (New York: Mentor Books, 1964), p. 18. We have insisted throughout that numbers belong with science rather than with metaphysics, and this is a case in point. Metaphysically speaking, one is a quality, not a number.

27. A pink unicorn is easy to conceive, however little we may expect to encounter one.

28. Wittgenstein's famous aphorism, "Whereof one cannot speak, thereof must one remain silent," can be read as this contention as aimed at speech and discursive thought. When Frank Ramsey added "and you can't whistle it either," he underscored the cutoff. The assertions are exceptionally crisp indices of one of the divides that separates contemporary from traditional

the fact that ultimates exceed the reach of our bread-and-butter faculties and can never be captured by minds that insist upon absolute rights of possession does not mean that these ultimates have no contact with the world we inhabit or with the human self in its totality. It is only because we invest all our interests in the specifiable, which to be such must perforce be partial and ephemeral, that no concern remains for that which is total and eternal and therefore unspecifiable. Even so, because it is total it cannot be escaped. The belief, normal to mankind, that meaning inheres in everything that exists and everything that happens derives at depth from the fact that the Ultimate, or Infinite as we are calling it, is omnipresent.

Being everywhere, it is, of course, in man; in the natural world it is in man preeminently. This takes us to our next chapter.

---

philosophy, for whereas traditional philosophy tried to suggest the in-expressible and alert men to its importance, recent Western philosophy has tried to eliminate it, though Late Heidegger east of the English Channel and Late Wittgenstein west of it are signs that the opposition may be softening. The just-quoted statement by Wittgenstein is from his early work, the *Tractatus*. Subsequently the ineffable became increasingly real for him, and though he did not retract his earlier contention that it cannot be specified propositionally—no mystic would have wanted him to retract this formulation of his point—he came to believe that the ineffable was embedded in the pattern of speech forms ("grammar") and in the fabric of human life in which these forms are woven. His later thought can be seen as a sustained effort to catch glimpses of the ineffable by penetrating life's ebb and flow through chinks in its linguistic texture.

He is the Self within and without; yea, within and without.

MAITRAYANA UPANISHAD, V.2

In truth I say to you that within this fathom-high body . . . lies the world and the rising of the world and the ceasing of the world.

THE BUDDHA

For the kingdom of Heaven, nay rather, the King of Heaven . . . is within us.

GREGORY PALAMAS

4. The Levels of Selfhood

As without, so within—the isomorphism of man and the cosmos is a basic premise of the traditional outlook. The preceding chapter mapped its cosmology; this one will consider the levels of reality as they appear within man himself. We could think of the chapter as an excursion into psychology were it not for the fact that that word as currently used denotes at best but half the ground to be covered: "pneumatology," the science of the soul or spirit, would be a better designation. A sentence by William James provides a bridge from psychology to the pneumatology we now essay.

The whole drift of my education goes to persuade me that the world of our present consciousness is only one out of many worlds of consciousness that exist, and that those other worlds must contain experiences which have a meaning for our life also; and that although in the main their experiences and those of this world keep discrete, yet the two become continuous at certain points, and higher energies filter in.[1]

1. *The Varieties of Religious Experience* (New York: Collier Books, 1961), p. 401.

If man does indeed mirror the cosmos, a quick review of the traditional cosmology will alert us to its regions that call for human counterparts. Visualized, that cosmology shows the earth, symbolic of the terrestrial sphere, enveloped by the intermediate sphere, which in turn is enclosed by the celestial, the three concentric spheres together being superimposed on a background that is Infinite.

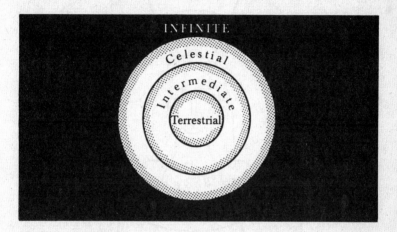

Considered in itself each sphere appears as a complete and homogeneous whole, while from the perspective of the area that encloses and permeates it, it is but a content. Thus the terrestrial world knows not the intermediate world, nor the latter the celestial, though each world is known and dominated by the one that exceeds and enfolds it.

Positioned, as we are, at the center of these realms, when we look out we look up, when we look in we look down. In the latter case empowering is sensed to erupt from below and proceed from within: vital organs are encased in skeletal armor, seeds slumber in husks, kernels are guarded by shells less animate (see figure on page 21). Chapter 2 described this inversion in a general way; now we are ready to delineate the echelons of selfhood that derive from and reflect the ontological planes the preceding chapter established. The overview can be diagrammed as follows:

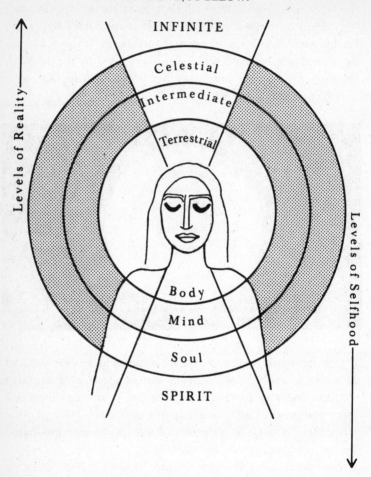

"AS ABOVE, SO BELOW."*

INFINITE

Celestial

Intermediate

Terrestrial

Body

Mind

Soul

SPIRIT

Levels of Reality ⟶

⟵ Levels of Selfhood

*The assertion is from *The Emerald Tablets of Hermes Trismegistus.*

1. Body

We begin with man's surface aspect, his body. One hundred fifty pounds, more or less, of protoplasm that we can see, touch, and maneuver, it is the most evident part of our makeup, so need not detain us long. Pages could be given to its wonders. We could describe the cells that are its building blocks, each equipped with hundreds or thousands of allosteric enzyme molecules a million billion times finer than the most delicate cybernetic relays man can devise. Or we could note the brain that is the body's apex; with its 10 billion neurons any one of which can be related to as many as 25,000 others for a number of possible associations that exceeds the number of atoms in the universe, it is the most highly organized three pounds of matter we know. There is no need to dwell on details.[2] We leap over them to consider the sentience that infuses the human frame.

2. Mind

Mechanists consider mind to be a part of the body, but this is a mistake. The brain is a part of the body, but mind and brain are not identical.[3] The brain breathes mind like the lungs breathe air.

It is not possible to prove these assertions, for as we just

2. No disrespect is intended the sciences that brought such facts to light or the scientists, inspired in investigation, ascetic in discipline, who discovered them. The point is only that size and complexity, however awesome they may appear until our minds get habituated to them, are consonant with reason and therefore are in principle unmysterious. This does not hold for the quarry we are tracking.

3. "Some say that we merely speak in two different languages when referring to thoughts on the one hand and to neural processes on the other. But we speak in two languages because we are talking of two different things. We speak of the thoughts Shakespeare had while writing his plays and not of the thoughts of hydrochloric acid dissolving zinc, because men think and acids don't." Michael Polanyi, *Personal Knowledge* (Chicago: The University of Chicago Press, 1958), pp. 389–90.

said, each plane when viewed from within presents itself as a complete and self-sufficient whole. But though this rules out the possibility of demonstrating the existence of ontological "mores" of whatever sort, intimations of such mores are likely to obtrude, for the lesser is in fact not self-contained. Whether a given individual picks up on these intimations—"hath ears to hear"—depends on his ontic sensitivity (see p. 50).

Intimations of the fact that the mind, though obviously implicated with the brain ("attached to the body" is Aristotle's wording) is not reducible to it are of three sorts.

First there is the evidence that derives from neurophysiologists themselves. A quarter-century ago when this science was getting on its legs, Sir Charles Sherrington wrote: "That our being should consist of two fundamental elements offers, I suppose, no greater improbability than that it should rest on one." The years that have intervened have not increased the improbability of the two-entities theory. On the contrary: Wilder Penfield, dean of living neurophysiologists if anyone deserves such a title, thinks that the advances the years have brought make the theory probable. In *The Mystery of the Mind: A Critical Study of Consciousness and the Human Brain,* he points out that by applying electrodes to the memory and motor regions of the cerebral cortex of patients undergoing brain surgery the surgeon can make them remember past events and move their bodily members, but there is no brain-spot which, if electrically stimulated, will induce patients to believe or to decide. Stressing that years of studying the mechanisms of the human brain have forced him to retain rather than abandon the distinction between mind and these mechanisms, Penfield concludes that:

> Mind must be viewed as a basic *element* in itself. . . . The mind seems to act independently of the brain in the same sense that a programmer acts independently of his computer. . . . It will always be quite impossible to explain the mind on the basis of neuronal action within the brain. . . . Mind comes into action and goes out of action with the highest brain-mechanism. But the mind has

energy [and] the form of that energy is different from that of neuronal potentials that travel the axone pathways.[4]

Still in the area of neurophysiology is the recent discovery that the two hemispheres of the human brain serve different functions. Its left hemisphere (which controls the right side of the body and perceives through right-body sense organs) works predominantly with the analytic, logical thinking of language and mathematics. Meanwhile the right hemisphere ("wired" to the left side of the body) proceeds holistically. Instead of following trails of linear reason and "single causation" as does the left hemisphere, it takes in fields in a gulp; it grasps intuitively, in patterned gestalts. It thinks, but because it bypasses language, it thinks tacitly in the sense in which Michael Polanyi uses this word in his *Tacit Dimension*. This mode of mentation equips it for artistic endeavor, pattern recognition —our ability to identify faces at a glance—and the orientation of our bodies in space: walking, swimming, or riding a bicycle. Since these right hemisphere functions involve space, whereas talk takes time, we can say that the right hemisphere functions predominantly spatially and the left temporally. If, as we are about to propose, the right hemisphere is in closer touch with the subtle plane than is the left, the following remark by a noted recent painter is precise: "Time is an invention of man, but space—space belongs to the gods" (Max Beckmann).

Since only the human brain is thus divided, no other species even prefiguring it, the division is obviously related to man's attendant monopoly, language. But why must linguistic competence be compartmentalized? Why does it not pervade the cerebral cortex as a whole? Because, it would seem, our entire

4. Princeton: Princeton University Press, 1975, pp. 81, 79, 80, 48. See also Sir John Eccles' Preface to Eric Polten, *Critique of the Psycho-Physical Identity Theory* (The Hague: Mouton, 1973), which is summarized in his own words as follows: "The program of the . . . materialists is . . . to reduce conscious experiences to the science of brain states and hence to physics. Thus everything would be reduced to properties of matter. Their efforts to deny or to ignore conscious experiences have collapsed because of its intrinsic absurdity" (p. ix).

being cannot be accommodated to it. This being the case, a part of the brain must be kept language-free. Only so can capacities that are incommensurate with language yet indispensable to life remain intact.

If it is impossible for man to manage the whole of his terrestrial life by means of language, it goes without saying that transverbal faculties must enter even more if he is to traffic with supraterrestrial planes, which differ in kind from the plane that language is primarily designed to cope with and mirror. Without empowerment by the psychic order, man cannot live: we see empirical evidence of this in the laboratory discovery that experimental subjects who are allowed to sleep but not to dream go mad; metaphysically it follows from the double fact that (a) the lesser is ordered and empowered by the greater, and (b) the psychic plane is greater than the corporeal. The psychic cannot, however, be fitted into corporeal categories which are also, in the main, the categories of language. Speaking in the manner of a Platonic myth, we might say that the mind, contemplating its descent into matter, foresaw that it would have to school itself in its ways. It did so by pouring its direct and luminous intellection into molds—concepts, words, language—that splintered it, for "rational" and "ratiocination" presuppose what the words suggest: a process in which we *ration* or divide up reality into separate things to facilitate discussion. In "the widest possible signification of the notion of sin, namely that of centrifugal movement" (F. Schuon), the mind consented to "take on the sins of the world" —the categories of matter and the language that in part reflects, in part creates, these categories. But if mind was to save the world—redeem it from total opacity and lifelessness—part of its nature had to remain outside those categories, for reason, being *founded* in distinctions, can at best only grope toward wholeness; indirectly through inference, and sequentially through time. The parallel with the two natures of Christ is exact: The mind assumes the conditions of the fall with its left (distinctively human) hemisphere while keeping its right hemisphere transcendent. That both hemispheres are requisite for man's full functioning is but one more evidence of his amphibious nature. He lives in the world while not being of it.

At the beginning of this section we said that there are three lines of argument that point toward the conclusion that mind exceeds the terrestrial plane. Neurophysiology we have noted; of the other two, one is theoretical and the other empirical.

The theoretical argument asks if matter can ever account for sentience, or mind in the widest sense of the word. This is a time-worn issue, of course, one of the thorniest in the entire history of philosophy. What we can say briefly is that no convincing materialistic explanation of mind has been forthcoming. Matter is located in space; one can specify precisely where a given tree, let us say, resides. But if one asks where his perception of the tree is located he can expect difficulties. The difficulties increase if he asks how tall his perception of the tree is; not how tall is the tree he sees, but how tall is his seeing of it. Conscious experience is, as Sir Charles Sherrington observed, "refractory to measurement."

> We cannot say that the experience of one light has twice the brightness of another. The terms in which we measure experience of sound are not terms of experience. They are terms of the stimulus, the physical sound, or of the nervous or other bodily action concomitant with the experience. . . . Mind, if it were energy, would be measurable quantitatively. . . . But . . . the search in [the energy-scheme] for a scale of equivalence between energy and mental experience arrives at none.[5]

That in some way I see because I have eyes and move my arms and legs because I want to seems as incontrovertible as anything can be; both our observation of life and the fact that within limits we can take it in hand and squeeze it like an orange presuppose body-mind interaction. But as to the char-

5. *Man on His Nature* (New York: Doubleday Anchor Books, 1953), p. 251.

acter of the interaction—Penfield says it is no more explicable today than it was in the time of Aristotle, but in reality it is less explicable, for Aristotle's nature included its subtle half whereas the current conception, which prunes nature to almost its quantifiable components, is less accommodating. As a consequence we live with an impasse. Sherrington's conclusion has lost nothing in the thirty-five years since he wrote it.

> Progress of knowledge . . . has only made more clear that the spatial concept's far-reaching notion "energy" is . . . powerless to deal with or to describe mind. . . . Mind . . . goes . . . in our spatial world more ghostly than a ghost. Invisible, intangible, it is a thing not even in outline; it is not a "thing". It remains without it forever.[6]

The matter comes to this: From the side of insentient matter the gulf that separates it from sentience is infinite; no bridge can reach the other bank. A ton of feathers presents no problem, but of items that weigh nothing whatever, no number will produce even an ounce. The doctrine of "emergent evolution" contributes nothing here. Proceeding from the fact that gases that cannot be poured may condense into liquids that can be poured, it argues that new qualities do arise. In riding such analogies it overlooks the fact that a clear continuity joins liquid to gas—the two are alternative arrangements of molecules in motion—whereas no common substratum linking sentience to insentience has been proposed. We shall return to the subject of emergence in Chapter 6. For now we note only that, as it happens, a substratum linking insentience to sentience does exist; depending on the level of reality on which the question is raised, it is form, existence, being, or the Infinite. But nothing answering to physical categories links the terrestrial plane to those above.

Such are the theoretical considerations that suggest that mind exceeds matter. A final line of argument is empirical. Instead of arguing that mind is a distinctive kind of entity,

6. *Ibid.*, p. 260.

it argues that it functions in distinctive ways. It plays by different rules, conforms to laws that differ in kind from those that matter exemplifies.

We are picking up here with the psi phenomena that were introduced in the preceding chapter: mental performances that are called parapsychological because by canons of the mind's usual operations they are scandalous. As was intimated in that chapter, we shall not try to prove that telepathy, clairvoyance, psychokinesis, and the like occur; volumes could be devoted to the project and still uncertainty would remain—in border areas ontological convictions count for more than do data, the latter being necessarily spotty when sighted from what might be called their underside on the ontological ladder. It is enough to note: (a) that some of the most recognized of modern intellects—men of the stature of Kant, Bergson, and William James—found the evidence in favor of parapsychology convincing; and (b) that the climate of opinion in general seems at present to be moving in the direction of credence: we recall the survey we earlier cited in which only 3 percent of the readers of *The New Scientist* reported that they consider psi phenomena to be impossible. Anyone who wishes his opinion to adhere as closely as possible to the evidence can look at Arthur Koestler's quick summary in his already-mentioned *The Roots of Coincidence*; if he has more time he might work through the two volumes of F. W. H. Myers's monumental *Human Personality and Its Survival of Bodily Death.*

So much for the existence of mind as a stratum of self that is neither reducible to the brain nor finally dependent on it. Turning to our experience of this stratum, we note that it takes two forms: waking and dreaming.

The "feel" of mind as we encounter it awake is so familiar that we overlook the mystery it parades in broad daylight. For on the one hand it truly reaches the physical world and no philosophical artifice can convince us of the contrary; meanwhile it consists of nothing but a tissue of images conditioned by what our senses can pick up, our interests induce them to pick up, and our past experience feeds in by ways of interpretations that elicit expectations. Everything that constitutes for us the world—its brute stubbornness, its continuity, its logical coherence—is a flow of phantasms, a gossamer of Berkeleian impressions. It is futile to try to know the world outside this magic lantern show, since it comes to us only through its "slides." All the while the world insists—and we cannot but agree—that we are not looking at a screen at all. The screen is a window through which we see the world itself, an autonomous order.

No theory of perception removes this miracle, the fact that an entity in one region of space flashes forth to assume—in truth *become*—the form (though not the matter) of entities removed: the sparkle in a mountain stream, the red on the throat of a ring-necked pheasant. Or causes those qualities to come to it—with mind we are on the intermediate plane where "wheres" cannot be pinpointed on the terrestrial map. When we move from perception to memory, imagination, and abstract thought the mysteries compound. If physiological psychology ever gives the impression of explaining these phenomena we should not be misled: it removes their mysteries in the way daylight banishes stars. Given sufficient pertinacity, reason's flailings can worry the mystery out of anything. In fact, of course, it is our sensibilities that die: " 'Tis ye, 'tis your estranged faces, That miss the many-splendoured thing." Alternatively, "It is not the eyes which grow blind. It is the hearts within the breasts that grow blind" (Koran, XXII, 46).

Daily, when we sleep, mind changes its register. In deep or dreamless sleep its content—assuming, with India, that it then continues to have a content[7]—is out of sight; presumably it is too undifferentiated to be recalled. Dreams, on the other hand, *can* be remembered, but we must not overlook the evaporation that occurs in the process. As we pass into wakefulness a sort of decantation takes place, of which we can, however, take

7. See Franklin Merrell-Wolff, *The Philosophy of Consciousness Without an Object* (New York: Julian Press, 1973).

note inasmuch as it is by degrees that a dream's force subsides and its otherworldliness eases into linguistic molds.

In dream the subtle body retires from the gross. The communication lines to its physical senses are disconnected, and it returns to its natural medium. For the duration of its "home leave" its pedestrian rendezvous with matter is suspended and it swims untrammeled in the psychic sphere. Because that sphere is its native habitat—the environment that is continuous with the stuff of which the mind is composed—the homecoming refreshes and restores. "He giveth his beloved—sleep."

Not that the dream world is more pleasant. Terrors lie in wait each time we turn out the light, nightmares being on average as common as dreams of peace. Nor do we see more clearly while asleep; if anything maya is compounded. We know less where we are and for this reason can take ourselves less in hand, a point the religions make by rating earthly life precious because of the opportunity it affords us to alter our condition toward final ends. Not pleasurableness but vividness and power are the respects in which dreams outrank our waking consciousness.

Dreams are invariably and by nature vivid because they know no habituation: each encounter with a rose or goblin is as if we were meeting it for the first time. As to power, the case is ambiguous. In one sense dreams have little power, for as we just noted, being disjoined from will, they do not in themselves affect our futures as much as our deliberate doings can. We cannot say that they have no power, for men have been known to emerge from dreams with perspectives that changed the course of their entire lives, as in Dostoevsky's story "The Dream of a Ridiculous Man." On the whole, however, the force dreams possess is passive rather than active; their emotional intensity is out of proportion to the difference they make. Beyond their freedom from habituation that has been remarked, their intensity derives from the fact that they put us in touch with forces that are more deep-lying and causative than the ones we notice in daily life. The dream lecture in the course of which I discover that I am prepared in neither content nor attire may be fictional with respect to real life— read: the waking world. Certainly I breathe easier when I awake and realize that it was, as I say to myself, only a dream. The fact remains that the anxiety the dream confronts me with is more real—calls more tunes, throws more switches in my moods and behavior—than the satisfaction I may feel later in the day in the course of an actual lecture for which I have prepared and donned trousers; in this sense we are indeed "such stuff as dreams are made on." Dream research has come up with exceptionally concrete evidence to document the fact that in dreams we are close to the center of life's vitalities. Eighty percent of the time men dream they have erections.

Between wakefulness and dreaming lies the twilight zone of daydream. Phenomenologists could dub in a whole landscape here, filled with phantasms that belie by their insubstantiality the power they exert over us. We will forgo the tour of this interface and touch instead on a final way we might catch a glimpse of the mind at work. If discarnates can indeed report through mediums their experiences after death, these reports would testify to the mind in an exceptionally pristine condition, a state totally unimplicated in the corporeal world. Such reports should be approached with great suspicion, for the "controls" in question are not integrated souls or even integrated minds; they consist at most of "psychic residues" that minds leave in their wake as they traverse the psychic plane.[8] When our bodies break up under the heavy years and our souls proceed toward eternity, superfluous fragments of our personalities may float on for awhile like small lost rafts on the psychic sea. Reports that derive from these fragments, assuming that some actually do so, could resemble the reports

8. This needs particularly to be said in this day of what our colleague Agehananda Bharati has called "rampant Rampaism," wherein the writings of an English plumber with the pen name Lobsang Rampa have produced a craze, as have those of Jane Roberts, who purports to be the amanuensis of a departed soul named Seth.

of schizophrenics: truth shot through with ellipses and masses of misrepresentation. From the reports of patients in our asylums a visitor from another planet might glean some sense of the earthly condition, but we would advise him against taking their reports at face value. The entire subject of spiritualism is so treacherous—René Guénon's *L'Erreur Spirite* sets it in perspective better than any other work we know—that we are tempted to skirt it entirely; but in order not to rule out the possibility that an occasional sliver of truth may reach us from these lands of shades via shamans or other mediums, we shall enter a single report, the latest as it happens to have come our way. Though we knew and respected the medium involved, Eileen Garrett, we quote her report, which purportedly came from Sir Arthur Conan Doyle, not for this reason but for one that is "logical"; that is, the extent to which it conforms to standard accounts of the intermediate plane.

I think that, as a matter of fact, when I say I am living in a world considerably like the one I have left, people will be surprised. I find myself doing many of the things which I did there. I find I am living in a world as dark as that which I have left, more's the pity. It is a country where pain is forever ended; where emotion is born a thousand times stronger; where inspirations reach me easier. I find myself in a bodily state. It is a world where the sinister life is to be dealt with. This is neither heaven nor hell. It is a combination of both. Believe me, it is only the beginnng. I understand that it tends to confirm the theory [that] soul goes through many phases. It is really the soul of me in bodily form. The scientists will disagree with me, but I am still "material," and so long as I am material, I feel myself the man I was on earth.[9]

We note in particular that the absence of physical pain and intensification of emotion conform to dream experience, and that the continuation of body in some form agrees with accounts that range from India's "subtle body" to the glorified and incorruptible "resurrected body" St. Paul alludes to.

9. Allan Angoff, *Eileen Garrett and the World Beyond the Senses* (New York: William Morrow & Co., 1974), pp. 40–41.

3. Soul

The conditions that govern this earthly cockpit in which we are stationed are local and relative. To daydream is to gaze out its windows at cloud kingdoms or stars so bright they seem at fingertip; at such times we forget for a spell our cabined condition and risk air's rhapsody of the deep. Sleep springs us from our carrier and brings the weightlessness of dream; death severs the lifeline to our transport, and for a time we stride the clouds like titans. "For a time," because there is a dimension of our selves that exceeds even the stratosphere, an essence no universe, subtle or gross, can contain. The ancients called it soul (*psyche, anima, sarira atman, nephesh,* or *nafs*) and though on the cosmological map it lies beyond the reach of the strongest telescope, we can join it in a twinkling once we learn its register. For it is closer to our essence by far than is the mind with which we usually identify.

The soul is the final locus of our individuality. Situated as it were behind the senses, it sees through the eyes without being seen, hears with the ears without itself being heard. Similarly it lies deeper than mind. If we equate mind with the stream of consciousness, the soul is the source of this stream; it is also its witness while never itself appearing within the stream as a datum to be observed. It underlies, in fact, not only the flux of mind but all the changes through which an individual passes; it thereby provides the sense in which these changes can be considered to be *his*. No collection of the traits I possess—my age, my appearance, what have you—constitutes the essential "me," for the traits change while I remain in some sense myself. To switch to the vocabulary of George Herbert Mead, the fragments of self that present themselves for identification constitute the "me" while the "I" that supports them as a clotheshorse supports the garments we drape over it remains concealed. To try to get the "I" into the field of vision is like trying to see my eyes by stepping back a pace; with every backward move I make, it retreats correlatively. But though the "me" is the only part of myself I can objectify, I sense it to be the object of a subject that is its source and superior.

This superior is the soul. We sense it indelibly in the incommunicable sense of what it feels like to be oneself instead of anyone else who has ever lived, but beyond this we know it only indirectly, by its effects. The way it supplies us with life is completely invisible, as is the way it directs the trajectory of our ontogenetic development: from the moment of conception it decrees that the raw materials the body assimilates in food and drink and air will be transformed according to incredible foreordinations to produce from among illimitable possibilities precisely—a human being. These workings of the soul are not only hidden from the subject they create; for the most part they elude even the laboratory scrutinies of science—microbiology gives only a barest glimpse of the drama involved. Where we do sense our souls is first, to repeat, in our discernment of our individuality—the fact that from conception to death we are the same person, which person is distinct from all others—and second, in our wants. For if we ask what we sense ourselves to be, there is no better initial answer than that we are creatures that want.

How far this definition holds for things other than human —animal, vegetable, possibly in some panpsychic sense even mineral—need not concern us. Nor need we lay out a classification that would set our wants in array: physical, psychological, spiritual, whatever. We cut through elaborations to center on a single point: the soul's essential dynamism.[10] In the faint glimpses of itself that the soul affords us, it appears less as a thing than as a movement; to paraphrase Nietzsche, it resembles a bridge more than a destination. Restlessness is built into it as a metaphysical principle. And though its reachings often seem random, they have a direction.

What is this direction?

Ever since man appeared on this planet he seems to have

10. "Self-motion is the very idea and essence of the soul." Plato, *Phaedrus*, 245d. "Anything that has a soul . . . move[s] itself." Aristotle, *Physics*, 265b, 34.

been searching for an object that he could love, serve, and adore wholeheartedly; an object which, being of the highest and most permanent beauty and perfection, would never permit his love for it to dwindle, deteriorate, or suffer frustration. The search has led to difficulties. It has brought him face to face with calamity and taken from him a toll of heavy sacrifice including the sacrifice of life itself. Yet he persists. The relentless urge of his nature compels him to continue at all costs. The entire history of the race—political, moral, legal, sociocultural, intellectual, economic, and religious, from earliest times to the present day—is the record of man's search for some beckoning object.

And again we ask, what is this object?

Freud thought it was connected in some way with sexual release, Adler with the drive for power. McDougall saw it as the urge to express the animal instincts that in man have entered into mysterious combination, Marx as economic well-being, often rationally disguised. The metaphysical answer is more basic. The soul is programmed, as we might say today, first to perpetuate its existence and then to augment it. Its tropism is toward being and its increase.

This is obvious in the case of drives like hunger and sex, but it holds for other outreaches as well, indeed for every outreach. We seek wealth and power because they strengthen our support system, fame and power because they increase our social stature. Friendship at once shores up our lives by the positive regard it elicits from others and enlarges our lives by stretching them, so to speak, to include the lives of others within them: we rejoice with those who rejoice and weep with those who mourn. Knowledge extends our understanding—"The world spreads out on either side / No wider than the mind is wide"—and beauty foretells the inner harmony of things. In the latter case, it is a quickening of spirit that signals augmented being rather than an enlargement in size, which is being's usual metaphorical quantifier.

Not that we see that being is invariably what we want. What the lover senses himself as wanting is his beloved. In this he is not mistaken, of course; the point concerns only *why* he loves her. That question the lover himself does not ask: immersed completely in the universe of love, its object is self-evidently its final cause. But if our object is to understand, the question "why" obtrudes. The beloved attracts because she configurates the precise aperture through which being can pour through to her lover in largest portions. Or change the image. Among innumerable pieces of quartz that lie strewn about the floor of a quarry it may chance that one alone bends the sun's rays at the exact angle that sends them toward my eyes. Doing so makes the quartz gleam. Yet it is the sun's light I see; were cloud to intervene, the quartz would turn to slag. So it goes: every emptiness we feel is "being" eclipsed, all restlessness a flailing for the being that we need, all joy the evidence of being found.

> Kings lick the earth whereof the fair are made,
> For God hath mingled in the dusty earth
> A draught of Beauty from His choicest cup.
> 'Tis *that*, fond lover—not these lips of clay—
> Thou art kissing with a hundred ecstasies,
> Think, then, what must it be when undefiled![11]

Even the addict who prowls the streets for his angry "fix" and the assassin who stalks his fated prey are reaching out for being. The alleys that they walk are blind ones; judged in terms of the larger being they preclude or the damage they work on the being of others they stand condemned. But if it were possible to consider the cocaine's "rush" by itself, apart from its consequences, it would be judged good; the same holds for the satisfaction that sweeps over the assassin as he effects his revenge. *Esse qua esse bonum est.* Being as being is good;[12] more being is better.

---

11. Jalal al-Din Rumi, *Mathnawi*, V, 372–75. English trans. by R. A. Nicholson, *Rumi, Poet and Mystic* (London: George Allen & Unwin, 1950), p. 45.

12. This is the metaphysical meaning in St. Paul's assertion to the Romans: "I know with certainty on the authority of the Lord Jesus that nothing is unclean in itself" (14:14).

It was Aristotle who saw every movement in the universe as ultimately caused by the irresistible attraction of being's superlative instance, the Unmoved Mover. *That* is the magnet; that, the far-off divine event toward which creation moves. St. Thomas detailed his insight: the dynamic pulse and throb of creation is the love of all things for the Infinite; in Dante's echo, it is "l'amor che muove il sole e l'altre stelle," the Love that moves the sun and the other stars. From the lowest level of reality, where even matter reaches out for form, to the highest heavens where angels gravitate around the Throne, a single breath and motion sweeps through existence, the search of each existent for the Good.

Our interest here is the way man, specifically his soul, instances this tendency. So sweetly are things disposed that it appears to the soul not so much that it is led as that it goes as it were of itself. Desiring self-fulfillment, it actively, of its own free will, goes where this fulfillment is to be found. And because the soul is finite, it appears to the soul as if its fulfillment were to be found in finite things: wealth, fame, power, a loved one, whatever. And again we say: in its way this is not inaccurate. But a telltale clue betrays the fact that such immediate objects of desire are but proximate ends that front for one that stands behind them and with respect to which they are but installments. This clue is the fact that we invest these manifestly finite objects with infinite worth. As infinite attractiveness is obviously not an objective property of our desired objects, a paradox ensues: we want infinitely, to the point of sacrificing our lives at times, things that are finite. Our usual way of explaining this paradox is to say that our evaluations are bestowed. The lover projects his estimate on the beloved—lays it on her, she may sometimes feel. The phenomenon admits of another interpretation. It is not so much that he projects infinity—infinite worth—upon her as that he glimpses infinity—the Infinite—through her. She has, for the duration that his passion lasts, become for him a symbol as (for Dante) was Beatrice: she in whom Heaven's glory walked the earth bodily. Symbols can be more or less effective and more or less durable, but within these limits they are the apertures we mentioned. However foolish the swain's love, while it lasts something, at least, of the Shekinah (Presence) hovers. God is near. The lover is in heaven.

For the most part the soul flits from symbol to symbol. Being flashes for a moment, now here, now there, only to withdraw. The object that admitted its light almost blindingly closes over, and we wonder, as we say, what we saw in *her*. In the long run the closures are providential, for they keep us from getting caught on ontological rungs that are incapable of satisfying us as much as ones that are higher.[13] At the time, however, the closures are painful. When no replacement appears, our inward indigence turns everything to wasteland; at this juncture macrocosm mirrors microcosm. Searching for a love that is unerodable, Plato depicted in the *Symposium* the possibility of passing from the love of beautiful objects to the love of that within these that makes them beautiful: from the love of a particular woman to the love of the femininity they have in common, to suggest an example that was not his. From this one might proceed, he argued, until one arrived at the love of the Good itself, whereupon, it being the Form that composes all lesser forms, one could in some respect love everything and so never be without an object for his affections.

For most temperaments this route is too abstract. Its alternative is to love not the Good but God. The object of this preference, as we pointed out in the preceding chapter, is not a fiction. On pain of anthropomorphism we must be on guard not to ascribe to God properties that make us distinctively human: our *kind* of knowledge, our *mode* of love. And we must not overlook that exceptional type of spiritual personality who, having sloughed off his own image and achieved within

13. "The desire for perfection . . . is that desire which always makes every pleasure appear incomplete, for there is no joy or pleasure so great in this life that it can quench the thirst in our Soul." Dante, *Il Convivio*, III. vi. 3.

himself a kind of total nudity, can know God otherwise than through a human prototype; this type we shall treat in the next section. But between anthropomorphism on the one river-bank and transpersonalism on the other flow the waters of the living God. It is not just, as we have noted, that the lion knows a leonine deity; that much was said in the preceding chapter. We must go further and say that what we see through the tinted glass of our finite human discernments is nonetheless there, and if an in-ways-humanized image serves as bridge to a region beyond the limitations under which all images must labor, then *al-hamdu lillah*—praise be to Allah, as the Muslims would say.

It is not easy to gauge the spiritual temperature of an age nor to discern the mode its spirituality assumes, but the prevalence of phrases like "the death of God" or better, "the eclipse of God," suggests that men seem to be "saying thou to the universe," to use William James's phrase, less than they did in the past, and hearing less in the way of personalized responses from it. Even entertainers capitalize on the point: "I needed God so I called him," a quipster remarks. "He put me on hold." It may be that the mechanization of our industrial environment—steel sheets and girders, concrete piers and asphalt roads, belching blast furnaces, heavy coal smoke, and dead neon signs—it may be that this enveloping insentience has led us unconsciously to assume that all environments are inanimate, whereas in fact, of course, above the smog the stars still shine and the angels sing. If deep is answering to deep less today it is not because the depths have changed, certainly not on their objective side. If our world has changed, this only reflects the change in the idea we now have of it. God has not retreated; it is we who have turned away.

So far have we strayed that we need a firsthand account to remind us what it was like to live in the conviction, periodically fortified by direct realization, that from beginning to end existence thrills to the life of the living God. To emphasize the fact that personalized experiences of God were not restricted to saints and seers, we deliberately present as illustration here an account by an anonymous layman, one drawn from the manuscript collection which the psychologist E. D. Starbuck assembled around the turn of the century.

I remember the night, and almost the very spot on the hilltop, where my soul opened out, as it were, into the Infinite, and there was a rushing together of the two worlds, the inner and the outer. It was deep calling unto deep—the deep that my own struggle had opened up within being answered by the unfathomable deep without, reaching beyond the stars. I stood alone with Him who had made me, and all the beauty of the world, and love, and sorrow, and even temptation. I did not seek Him, but felt the perfect unison of my spirit with His. The ordinary sense of things around me faded. For the moment nothing but an ineffable joy and exultation remained. It is impossible fully to describe the experience. It was like the effect of some great orchestra when all the separate notes have melted into one swelling harmony that leaves the listener conscious of nothing save that his soul is being wafted upwards, and almost bursting with its own emotion. The perfect stillness of the night was thrilled by a more solemn silence. The darkness held a presence that was all the more felt because it was not seen. I could not any more have doubted that *He* was there than that I was. Indeed, I felt myself to be, if possible, the less real of the two.[14]

Happiness, it is said, has no history. History recounts wars and plagues and famines. All the while on the underside of its mantle of disaster a different kind of drama has never ceased from being woven. A private, interior drama consisting of scenes like the one just described, it reaches the pages of history only when it makes an exceptional impact, as did St. Paul's experience on the Damascus road or Luther's sudden comprehension of the full import of "I believe in the forgiveness of sins." Yet precisely because it is an interior drama it touches the wellsprings of joy and resiliency. Those who are tapped for its cast can lie down on nettles, lie down with vipers, and

14. Quoted in James, *Varieties of Religious Experience*, p. 69.

scarcely notice where they are. The world is not relinquished, but it assumes its proper place. It

>   is not all;
> Is harsh with envy, greed, assault,—or blooms
> With friendship, courage, truth, is beautiful;
> Yet is at best but an inn on a thoroughfare:
> *Provincial*, one might call the mind contented there.[15]

The phenomenology of the soul's romance with its Creator admits of three distinguishable modes. In the first the accent falls on the love the soul feels for God. The troubadours come to mind here, as do the seekers of the grail and the seventh- to ninth-century Alvars of South India, *alvar* meaning literally "diver" (into the ocean of divine consciousness). These ecstatic devotees of Vishnu pressed into devotional service the entire complement of human emotions, from the tenderness of a doting mother to the terror of an abandoned child, but it was in the half-crazed, near-hysterical longing of a lover for his absent love that their fervor reached its peak:

> When will the time come when I shall see Him without inter-mission and place my crowned head at His feet? When will the time come when my tears of ecstasy shall flow on seeing the wonderful Lord? When will the time come when my mind gazing at His moon-like face will melt into Him?
>
> *Kulasekhara Alvar*

A favorite allegory in Sufi tales concerns the shaikh who abdicates his eminence in the world and to the incomprehension and disgust of those who had envied and respected him now lives only to gain the company of some simple wench who has won his heart. His beard mats up and his clothes become rags, for his thoughts are so completely on her that none remain for his own person. Even death is no deterrent, for whereas her continued absence is intolerable, in her presence he could die in peace.

15. Edna St. Vincent Millay, *Conversation at Midnight* (Harper and Brothers, 1937), p. 30.

In the second mode, the accent falls on God's love for man. Posit a lover whose existence has centered for months in an anguished and unrequited yearning like that of the shaikh just depicted. Though his passion is spurned he nevertheless longs for nothing so much as to be in his beloved's presence: in her absence he consoles himself with recollections of the times he was with her and anticipations of ones when he will see her again. If after months of such seemingly hopeless longing the swain were to find that the princess was beginning to take an interest in him, could we imagine his state? Not only does he want, he is wanted; not only does he love, he is loved. And should it transpire that from a modest beginning the princess's regard for him were to rise to an intensity that rivaled his own —the intensity of his desperation when it seemed that his love was hopeless and of his rapture when it began to look as if it were not—would we then be able to follow his emotions to their Himalayan heights? It is on record that such are the emotions that visit the soul when it discovers that it is literally loved by the God who made and rules the universe. The following is the account of Mrs. Jonathan Edwards:

> Last night was the sweetest night I ever had in my life. I never before, for so long a time together, enjoyed so much of the light and rest and sweetness of heaven in my soul. . . . Part of the night I lay awake, sometimes asleep, and sometimes between sleeping and waking. But all night I continued in a constant, clear, and lively sense of the heavenly sweetness of Christ's excellent love, of his nearness to me, and of my dearness to him; with an inexpressibly sweet calmness of soul in an entire rest in him. I seemed to myself to perceive a glow of divine love come down from the heart of Christ in heaven into my heart in a constant stream, like a stream or pencil of sweet light.[16]

In our analogy we spoke of the princess's love as rivaling the swain's, but in the present case God's love exceeds the soul's, for the soul is finite, with the consequence that what is total

16. Quoted in James, *Varieties of Religious Experience,* p. 223.

for it is no match for the love that flows from a source that is illimitable. It must have been this sense—the sense that the Lord of all Being loved them with a strength that exceeded their own, loved to the point of sacrificing his very Son for them—that empowered the early Christians to launch what numerically was to become the foremost religion in the world.

The third and final element in the phenomenology of the soul's encounter with God emerges as we continue with Mrs. Edwards's account, which was interrupted. After describing her sense of God's love streaming toward her like a pencil of light, she writes:

> At the same time my heart and soul all flowed out in love to Christ, so that there seemed to be a constant flowing and reflowing of heavenly love, and I appeared to myself to float or swim, in these bright, sweet beams, like the motes swimming in the beams of the sun, or the streams of his light which come in at the window. I think that what I felt each minute was worth more than all the outward comfort and pleasure which I had enjoyed in my whole life put together. It was pleasure, without the least sting, or any interruption. It was a sweetness, which my soul was lost in; it seemed to be all that my feeble frame could sustain. . . .
>
> As I awoke early the next morning, it seemed to me that I had entirely done with myself. I felt that the opinions of the world concerning me were nothing, and that I had no more to do with any outward interest of my own than with that of a person whom I never saw. The glory of God seemed to swallow up every wish and desire of my heart.[17]

For our present purpose the principal point of this passage is contained in its opening sentence, which registers the sense of "a constant flowing and reflowing of heavenly love." Whereas in the first mode the accent was on man's love for God and in the second on God's love for man, the two are now equalized in full reciprocity. Yet more than reciprocity; in identity. In what, at risk of indignity, we are tempted to call a love loop— Dionysius calls it the "unerring revolution"—the soul per-

17. *Ibid.*

ceives that the love it directs toward God is none other than that which originated in God's love for it. It is the selfsame love, turned back on its point of origin—in the moment when Dante sees Beatrice in the way that transfigures his life forever, he sees her as God sees her, her and everything that is. Plotinus saw this point: "The fullest life is the fullest love, and the love comes from the celestial light which streams forth from the Absolute One" (*Enneads*, VI.7.23). Ibn 'Arabi makes the point as well:

> The soul . . . "sees" God not through itself, but through him; it loves only through Him, not by itself. . . . The soul is *His* organ of perception. [The soul's] sympathy with being is . . . the passion [God's] Presence arouses in the soul. Accordingly it is not by itself or even in conjunction with Him that the soul contemplates and loves, but through Him alone. . . . The soul is His organ. . . . It is He who seeks and is sought for, He is the Lover and He is the Beloved.[18]

St. John of the Cross says the same. Of the advanced state in which the soul is seized by the love of God he writes:

> The principal agent . . . is God. For God secretly and quietly infuses into the soul loving knowledge and wisdom without any intervention of specific acts [on the soul's part]. The soul has then to walk . . . conducting itself passively, and having no diligence of its own but possessing this simple, pure and loving awareness.[19]

According to Ruysbroeck, "The love of God is an outpouring and an indrawing tide."

Our account of the soul, the theme Plato esteemed to be "of large and more than mortal discourse" (*Phaedrus*, 246a), is complete. Having identified its essential tendency as "that veritable love, that sharp desire" (Plotinus) and its final object as Being, if one thinks "abstractly," or God in his personal

---

18. Henry Corbin, *Creative Imagination in the Sufism of Ibn 'Arabi* (Princeton: Princeton University Press, 1969), pp. 151–52.

19. *The Complete Works of St. John of the Cross*, trans. by Allison Peers (London: Burns, Oates and Washbourne, Ltd., 1934), Vol. III, pp. 76–77.

mode if one does not, the way is clear to move to the final rung on the scale of reality and the deepest element in man. But lest it be inferred from this projected move that we do not take the soul's God seriously, that we regard him as no more than an edifying fiction or symbol,[20] we close this section with words that count the more because written by the man who more than any other has secured for us the personal God without loading him with finality—the two things must be said together. Speaking of the levels within the self and the ascending importance of those which, lying deeper, are more substantial, Frithjof Schuon writes:

> According to some people, it is enough to convince oneself, as it were by auto-suggestion, that one is neither the body nor the mind. This truth is not realizable, however, until body and mind have conformed on their plane to what may be called the "Divine Will"; one cannot attain *Atma* without God or in opposition to God. The "personal Divinity" only allows those who adore Him to understand that He is not the absolute Reality.[21]

We can see why this is so. To identify (merge) with what is pitted against us (feared and resented) is out of the question; only love can draw us, first toward, and then into, another. Only when the demandingness of separative existence (the *tanha*-craving of body and mind) has fallen away, leaving us identified with the region of self that loves its matrix and knows its love to be reciprocated—only selves that are living at this barely separate level can think of taking the final step

20. He is not a symbol. Or to speak precisely, only with respect to the plane above him does he serve as symbol. Viewed in relation to God's infinite mode his personal mode does point beyond itself. On its own plane, the celestial, it exists without qualification, and we must remember that the reality of that plane vastly exceeds our own. On our own plane the representations we attempt of God have inevitably a symbolic element inasmuch as they can never rise to be their object's equal, but this does not keep them from being literally true in certain respects, as when they assert that God exists and that the degree of his existence exceeds our own. Symbolism is the science of the relationship between different levels of reality (Ghazali) and cannot be precisely understood without reference thereto.

21. Frithjof Schuon, *The Language of the Self* (Madras: Genesh & Co., 1959), pp. 54–55.

of relinquishing their individuality entirely, if "thinking" has any application in a state that is on the verge of simply dissolving into the Godhead. As long as the sense of separateness continues, which is to say in some degree until death, the self must love and worship the Other its life confronts, for to repeat, this is the only attitude (affective stance) that can counter the alienation of separateness and cause it to diminish. To the degree that a soul worships, it does not demand to be "I," and so is not opposed in principle to the thought, should it arise, that "I am not my finite self; I am the Atman." It is in this way that an adoring soul is the only possible bridge to Spirit.

4. Spirit

If soul is the element in man that relates to God, Spirit is the element that is identical with Him—not with his personal mode, for on the celestial plane God and soul remain distinct, but with God's mode that is infinite. Spirit is the Atman that *is* Brahman, the aspect of man that *is* the Buddha-nature, the element in man which, exceeding the soul's full panoply, is that "something in the soul that is uncreated and uncreatable" (Eckhart). It is the true man in Lin Chi the Ch'an master's assertion that "beyond the mass of reddish flesh is the true man who has no title"; and the basis for the most famous of Sufi claims: Mansur al-Hallaj's assertion, *"ana'l-Haqq*, I am the Absolute Truth, or the True Reality."

We speak of identity, and this is right, for on this final stratum the subject-object dichotomy is transcended. Still, man's finitude remains, which means that the identity must not be read simplistically. Spirit is Infinite, but man is finite because he is not Spirit only. His specifically human overlay—body, mind, and soul—veils the Spirit within him. As the Jains say, a lamp's flame may be bright, but let its chimney be coated with dust or soot and the lamplight will be dim. Spirit's presence in man does not render him omnipotent or omniscient, nor relieve him of limitations that dog even the greatest saints: "Why callest me good? there is none good but one, that is, God" (Matt. 19:17). But though it does not render man omnipotent, Spirit does, as we might put the matter, remove his impotence.[22] It does so by providing him with a vantage point from which he can see that his station requires the limitations his humanity imposes. By itself that realization would produce only resignation, but the something in man that enables him to see that he must be limited also does the limiting, if we may use this perhaps curious way of registering the fact that the Infinite cannot tolerate a second of its kind: some things are obvious. Spirit decrees that body, being corporeal, must naturally be limited. Man accepts that decree for his physical component; for his mind and soul as well, in their respective ways. Meanwhile his Spirit remains free, it being the sovereign that imposes the decree rather than the prisoner who submits to it.

The shifting of the ballast of man's self-recognition from servant to Sovereign proceeds by stages. Following a Sufi formulation, we may distinguish between the Lore of Certainty, the Eye of Certainty, and the Truth of Certainty, the first being likened to hearing about fire, the second to seeing fire, and the third to being burned by fire. Spirit is the bedrock of our lifestream, but the waters that course over it are for the most part too roiled to allow the bed to be seen. Where the banks widen and the current slows, however, sediment settles and we glimpse our support. Always in this life some water intervenes to veil, but at the moment the point is the opposite one. Not only is the bed there throughout; it is truly the bed that we see even when we see it obscurely. Man is Spirit while not Spirit unalloyed.

Back now to Lin Chi's "true man who has no title" residing

22. "When my life opens up very clearly, I can't help, from the depths of my heart, wanting to bow. When the mind that wants to bow to enemies and friends and demons and gods and evils and Buddhas and good friends and bad people—when this feeling comes tumbling out of my deep life, then *I am already master of the whole world, I control the entire world*, I become friends with all human and other beings." Hara Akegarasu, "O New Year!" *Zen Notes*, XXII, 1 (Jan. 1975), 3 (italics added).

beyond the mass of reddish flesh. He has no title—is not man or woman, young or old, rich or poor—because as we spelled out at some length in the preceding chapter, the Infinite which Spirit overlaps defies positive characterization. Since "Spirit" and "Infinite" are, like "Atman" and "Brahman," but two words for a single reality, we summarize what was said about it under the caption "The Infinite." Though it is possible to intuit it directly, we can think of it only by invoking a double negative. Peripherally Spirit is without boundaries; internally it is without barriers. It knows neither walls that encompass nor walls that divide.

Between thought (which proceeds indirectly through concepts) and intuition (which directly identifies) lies a middle ground. We scarcely know what to call it. Symbolism? Art in its sacred sector? It uses the stones of earth to raise on its flatlands spires that point toward heaven. This middle mode of concourse plays while logic works. It is unquestionably alert, while being in some respects passive to the point of dissociation, for to shift gears an engine must disengage and pass through neutral. Playing with the second of the above stipulations about spirit—its indifference to internal divisions—we note first that it is possible for nondifferentiation to climb to the point where the world's divisions vanish completely. Ramakrishna reports his experience of this condition as follows:

> Suddenly the blessed Mother revealed Herself. The buildings with their different parts, the temple, and everything else vanished from my sight, leaving no trace whatsoever, and in their stead I saw a limitless, infinite effulgent Ocean of Consciousness. As far as the eye could see, the shining billows were madly rushing at me from all sides with a terrific noise, to swallow me up! What was happening in the outside world I did not know; but within me there was a steady flow of undiluted bliss.[23]

But though corporeal distinctions can be thus erased, the instances in which they are erased constitute an exceptional

23. Nikhilananda, *Ramakrishna: Prophet of New India* (New York: Harper and Brothers, 1948), pp. 9–10.

class. Normally distinctions remain but are softened. Or they remain precise while changing from barriers to bridges.

> "I," table, flower, fragrance, the chirping of birds, are all un-deniably present, but being in reality nonexistent they do not present themselves as solid, self-subsistent entities. They are trans-parent and permeable. Reflecting each other, interpenetrating each other, and dissolving themselves into each other, they form an integral whole which is nothing other than the direct appearance of the primary level of Reality. In this sense, sensible perception, wherein distinctions loom so large, is reduced almost to nullity. It loses its functional basis, it does not work properly, in the presence of the trans-subjective and trans-objective awareness of the inter-fusion of all things where "gnat," instead of presenting itself as an independent external entity, means rather its identification with Being and all other things so that they end up by being fused into one.[24]

In and through the body and *ahamkara* (ego sense) of every human being Lin Chi's man with no title is untiringly alive. He is not the personal God; he is the all-embracing Infinite. He is the actor who has internalized the play so completely that he identifies more with it than with his role in it: he will make the audience despise him if the play requires that he do so. We can generalize this image. Every figure presupposes a ground against which it is seen or thought. But since in the final analysis the individual could not exist without its ground or be conceived without presupposing it, the two are—in last analysis, we repeat—inseparable. In a way that is absolutely crucial, a thing's ground is an aspect of the thing itself. Seen with the "eye of the heart," the organ of spiritual vision, this body of flesh and blood which in corporeal respects is frail as foam, fleeting as dew, is at the same time, in this very moment and on this very spot, the infinite and eternal Life instancing itself in this particular respect. Normally, as we have noted, the perception does not involve the total dissolu-tion of finitude in the ocean of Godhead. Rather it is the

24. Adapted from the writings of Toshihiko Izutsu.

experience of finitude *as* infinity, or temporality *as* eternity, the opposites blended in ineffable yet palpable whole. It is as if an iceberg were suddenly to realize that it is H_2O.[25]

The fact that the notion of the Infinite appeals to us is itself evidence of Spirit's reality, for metaphysical arguments would never convince were there not within us a trace of that which they set out to communicate—if the certainty they seek to awaken were not already sleeping in the substance of our souls. At the same time we resist the notion, for it requires that we shift our identification from the parts of our being that press palpably upon us. The writing of this chapter happened to span a Christmas in which there was a two-year-old in the house, and it became evident again how strong the *ahamkara* or ego sense is ingrained within us. One had remembered from one's own children the insatiability of the ego's wants: the Christmases when what counted was not what the presents were but their quantity, with the inevitable tears when the number proved finite. It took a grandchild, however, to revive the memory of an earlier stage when the life task was to firm up the sense of selfhood itself. At this state not even numbers mattered as much as who the numbers were for. Before each present was opened, it was imperative that it be paraded and acknowledgment secured from each person assembled that "This is *my* present. This present is *mine!*" The sands of the Sahara, and a grain pops up to announce: I exist!

Once personal identity is established the issue shifts to what

25. The image of ice and water "is all the truer in that the frozen crystalisation appears to be far more substantial than unfrozen water; and yet when a large piece of ice melts the result is a surprisingly small quantity of water. Analogously the lower worlds [the terrestrial and intermediate planes], for all their seeming reality, depend for their existence upon a relatively unample Presence compared with that which confers on the Paradises [the celestial plane] their everlasting bliss; yet here again, ever-lastingness is not Eternity, nor are the joys of these Paradises more than shadows of the Absolute Beatitude of the Supreme Paradise [the Infinite]." Martin Lings, *What Is Sufism?* (Berkeley: University of California Press, 1975), pp. 70–71.

that identity is to be attached to. An eighth birthday and the boy was happy until he went to bed and the light was out. Then, in the aloneness of the dark, time paid him its first visit, whispering that he would never be seven again. And the prospect was intolerable. Since seven was what the boy sensed himself to be, the day that had just ended being insufficient to offset his identification with the plans and projects of the days and weeks that had preceded it, time's notice fell as death warrant. The death of himself-as-seven was the death of *him*, the only "him" that at the time was in view. He jumped from his bed and ran to his parents sobbing, "Take the presents back; I don't want them. I just want to be seven."

We smile at the boy's naïveté, but we know what he meant. For with the exception of those supernatural moments when reality breaks through the carapace of time like lightning and reveals the landscape in which we *are* infinite, every human has his age seven, his less than total self, with which he myopically identifies. The referent is elastic. An addict while his tissues scream knows himself as little more than a demanding body. At the other end of the spectrum are the times when one's cup runs over to the point where it would be easy to lay down one's life if the need arose. But almost invariably there is some point where selfhood is sensed to end and the not-self begin. This not-self, too, can be variously viewed: it can appear as a predominantly hostile world of alien objects and circumstances that kick and buffet, or as everlasting arms from whose embrace it is impossible to fall. One must come to the point where they are seen as the latter before one can take the final step in self-abandonment and identify with one's surround, which is why the preceding section asserted that the door that leads from soul to spirit is the door of love: love of Being-as-a-whole or of the God who is its Lord. For Spirit to permeate the self's entirety, the components of the self must be aligned: body in temperance, mind in understanding (Gautama's Right Views), and soul in love. But the immediate point is that even when the environment is seen to be benign, as long as it presents itself as distinct and other there will be imponderables which must be written off to God's inscrutable ways. The only alternative is to remove the dichotomy itself.

The removal is effected by perceiving the "other" as one's destiny. As we despair of equaling a formulation of this point that has come our way, we quote it at some length.

There is no radical distinction to be made between what a man is given in the way of mind, emotional make-up and body on the one hand and, on the other, what he is given in the way of outward circumstances and environment. Together they form a significant whole and all are aspects of a particular individual life. The being between birth and death scrawls—in matter and in events—a pattern which, taken as a whole, expresses his unique identity. This man, So-and-So, is not a sealed personality moving through an alien environment. He is the sum total of all that he does and all that happens to him and all that comes within his range, spread out (from our point of view) in time and space, but a single, timeless fact in the mind of God. What we are and where we are cannot ultimately be divided. And to accept our destiny is to accept ourselves, recognizing that what happens to us is as much a part of our nature—in the widest sense—as the most intimate contours of our own selfhood. It is sometimes said that the fatal bullet has its victim's name upon it and fits no other flesh.

In the last resort, a man looks at the love or anger or fear within himself and says, So this is me. Looks at his withered hand or wounded foot and says, So this is me. Looks at the woman he has married or the garden he has planted and says, So this is me. Looks finally upon his enemy and upon his death and says, So this is me. But in saying this he bears witness to the fact that he is also incomparably more than an itemised list of the elements that make up his individuality and its inseparable field of action.

And in acknowledging so much that is a part of ourselves (since our boundaries extend to the furthest horizons we can see from our particular vantage point) we make an act of recognition which actualises what was inherent in us from the start—almost as though we existed only to discover what was always there—recognising our name-tag on everything that comes our way. But the part of us that is our destiny, streaming in upon us in the form of "out-side" events through the course of time, can be recognised as belonging to our own particular pattern only when it has happened. The religious man can say, "Thy will be done!" as a statement of his intention to accept this will when it has been done and is apparent to him, but it is not our nature to be able to foresee the future except under the most unusual circumstances. In general, acceptance of destiny is acceptance of what has happened, not of what might happen (but might be prevented).[26]

Assuming that the acceptance in question is in the mode of affirmation and not solely resignation, acceptance of one's destiny as part of one's selfhood is an aspect of that love of being or God that opens us to the Infinite. But enough: the point has been made or it will not be made here. We close the chapter with a Sufi tale, "The Tale of the Sands," that epitomizes what this section has tried to say.

A stream, from its source in far-off mountains, passing through every kind and description of countryside, at last reached the sands of the desert. Just as it had crossed every other barrier, the stream tried to cross this one, but it found that as fast as it ran into the sand, its waters disappeared.

It was convinced, however, that its destiny was to cross this desert, and yet there was no way. Now a hidden voice, coming from the desert itself, whispered: 'The Wind crosses the desert, and so can the stream.'

The stream objected that it was dashing itself against the sand, and only getting absorbed: that the wind could fly, and this was why it could cross a desert.

'By hurtling in your own accustomed way you cannot get across. You will either disappear or become a marsh. You must allow the wind to carry you over, to your destination.'

But how could this happen? 'By allowing yourself to be absorbed in the wind.'

This idea was not acceptable to the stream. After all, it had never been absorbed before. It did not want to lose its individuality.

26. Gai Eaton, "Man as Viceroy," *Studies in Comparative Religion*, Autumn 1973, pp. 239–40.

And, once having lost it, how was one to know that it could ever be regained?

'The wind,' said the sand, 'performs this function. It takes up water, carries it over the desert, and then lets it fall again. Falling as rain, the water again becomes a river.'

'How can I know that this is true?'

'It is so, and if you do not believe it, you cannot become more than a quagmire, and even that could take many, many years; and it certainly is not the same as a stream.'

'But can I not remain the same stream that I am today?'

'You cannot in either case remain so,' the whisper said. 'Your essential part is carried away and forms a stream again. You are called what you are even today because you do not know which part of you is the essential one.'

When he heard this, certain echoes began to arise in the thoughts of the stream. Dimly, he remembered a state in which he—or some part of him, was it?—had been held in the arms of a wind. He also remembered—or did he?—that this was the real thing, not necessarily the obvious thing, to do.

And the stream raised his vapour into the welcoming arms of the wind, which gently and easily bore it upwards and along, letting it fall softly as soon as they reached the roof of a mountain, many, many miles away. And because he had had his doubts, the stream was able to remember and record more strongly in his mind the details of the experience. He reflected, 'Yes, now I have learned my true identity.'

The stream was learning. But the sands whispered: 'We know, because we see it happen day after day: and because we, the sands, extend from the riverside all the way to the mountain.'

And that is why it is said that the way in which the Stream of Life is to continue on its journey is written in the Sands.[27]

27. Idres Shah, *Tales of the Dervishes* (New York: E. P. Dutton, 1970), pp. 23–24.

5. The Place of Science

The modern West is the first society to view the physical
world as a closed system. It is customary for those who protest
this view to do so by parading the dire consequences that it
has occasioned, but this will not be our tack—not, we hasten
to say, because we think that it is mistaken but because we
do not know if it is or not. In principle every charge that can
be made against modernity—and by now who does not know
them by heart?—can be matched by an equal indictment of
antiquity: Hitler by Attila, Auschwitz by Egypt's burial of
live slaves with their pharaohs, and Rome's use of Christians
for human torches. Who can not see the Nazi in all history?
To cut through the balance of charge and countercharge
requires instinct, an intuitive sense of how it has felt to live
in alternative societies, and this sense we confess we lack.
True, a logical point announces itself now and again, asking
if the prospect of an infinite and eternal beatitude which the
traditional perspective held out to man would not have exer-
cised on balance a leavening influence, but this is the note of
a distant horn, too faint to be heard in argument. Our
objection to regarding the physical world as a closed system is
not that the view is unfortunate but that it is untrue. To ask
whether to believe what is untrue can in the long run be
fortunate is again to turn thought toward pragmatic waters,
and we refuse to be diverted.

This book opened by saying that it was modern science that
reduced the West's view of reality to its material stratum—
not science itself, but an unwarranted conclusion that its

spectacular success engendered: the conclusion that no strata other than the one science connects with exist. It is now time to turn the tables and ask if, once it is relieved of this unwarranted appendage, science does not stand in *supporting* relation to the traditional outlook. The most interesting version of the question is: Can science itself remain housed in being's basement? but since this version must be answered by scientists themselves, we content ourselves with a weaker variant. Not, Does science require transphysical domains? but rather, Does it hint of their existence? will be the question for us here.

The point is this: Science, like most things, has two sides. If one takes what turns up on its viewfinder as exhaustive of reality, the consequence (as we have seen) is scientism and the materialism it argues. If, on the other hand, one begins by realizing what Chapter 1 argued is now almost a closed case, namely that the viewfinder is in principle limited, one then looks at science for clues as to the nature of what lies outside it. Clues are not proofs, of course, but they are something, and to follow their lead is the present chapter's object. If "a symbol is something in a lower 'known and wonted' domain which the traveller considers not only for its own sake but also and above all in order to have an intuitive glimpse of the 'universal and strange' reality which corresponds to it in each of the hidden higher domains,"[1] anything, as we have noted more than once, can qualify. Even science. If Allah "has not disdained to use even the gnat as symbol" (Koran), there is nothing unlikely in the notion that man's brightest intellectual exploit may likewise house meanings beyond those it wears on its sleeve.

What are these meanings as they bear on the human spirit?

They show themselves in a series of parallels between science and religion. Both claim that: (1) Things are not as they seem; (2) the other-than-the-seeming is a "more"; indeed, a stupen-

1. Abu Bakr Siraj Ed-Din, *The Book of Certainty* (New York: Samuel Weiser Inc., 1970), pp. 50–51.

dous more; (3) this more cannot be known in ordinary ways; (4) it can, however, be known in ways appropriate to it; (5) these appropriate ways require cultivation; (6) and they require instruments. We proceed, now, to detail these parallels.

1. Things Are Not As They Seem

One of the upshots of modern science has taken the form of an exposé: it has unmasked the claims of man's sense receptors to disclose the world as it actually is. My senses tell me that the desk I am leaning on is solid. Not so, says science; if I could shrink to the size of an electron I would see that it is mostly empty: the ratio of matter to space in it is on the order of a baseball in a ballpark. Or my senses tell me that the desk is static. Wrong again, says physics; it is a hive of activity with electrons circling their nuclei a million billion times a second, or (in undulatory terms) with electrons vibrating more times each second than the number of seconds that have elapsed since the earth's crust was formed. The desk is compacted power—closer to pure energy than to the lifeless block my hands and eyes report. These are, of course, but samples. Wherever we turn, our senses bounce back fictions. It is not just that they do not inform us of nature's mien; they are expressly devised not to inform us. Had they presented us with the way things are we could not have survived. If we perceived atoms or quanta instead of cars we would be run over. Had our ancestors seen electrons instead of bears they would have been eaten.

We now swing into this chapter's central exercise: to place beside each of the points about science that we list its counterpart in the traditional (as opposed to modern), religious (as opposed to secular), or humanistic (as opposed to scientistic) outlook; in this book the three adjectives are largely synonymous. Anticipating physics' discovery that our senses deceive is the traditional claim that our sensibilities mislead. No more than man's unaided senses disclose the nature of the physical universe do his standard sensibilities discern the world's import: the meaning of life, history, or existence in general. "Eye hath not seen, nor ear heard . . . the things which God hath prepared" (I Cor. 2:9). To which C. S. Lewis adds:

> Christianity claims to be telling us about another world, about something *behind* the world we can touch and hear and see. You may think the claim false; but if it were true, what it tells us would be bound to be difficult—at least as difficult as modern physics, and for the same reason.[2]

Sufi tales almost invariably turn on a double reading of events; at a decisive turn in the story the ordinary perception of what has transpired is countered by an alternative that spins the situation around and shows it in a light that is diametrically opposite to the one that had prevailed. It is the "fool" who turns out to have been wise; the trinket, bought for a song and soon discarded, is in fact made of pure gold; the man who is ignored because he is dressed in rags is the king in disguise. You never know! The Indian doctrine of maya generalizes the point. The life that we see is a tissue of misreadings. He "saw life steadily and saw it whole," wrote Matthew Arnold of Sophocles. To a degree, perhaps, but who really attains this height? In exactly the way that our eyes are blind to all but the limited band of lightwaves they are tuned to, our hearts disregard events that lie outside their own self-interest. Moreover, the fashioned worlds that we do see and feel are governed by laws of perspective: objects close at hand seem bigger than those that are distant, and events of the moment more important than those of tomorrow. "So teach us to number our days, that we may apply our hearts unto wisdom" (Ps. 90:12). What a curious prayer—that we be taught that we must die! Who doesn't know that? we say, until on reflection we realize that no one knows it, not in a way that enables him to live each day as if it were his last.[3]

2. Condensed from *The Problem of Pain* (New York: The Macmillan Company, 1943).

3. "Of all the world's wonders, which is the most wonderful?"
"That no man, though he sees others dying all around him, believes that he himself will die" (*Mahabharata*).

Monks keep skulls on their tables to help them remember.

Maya derives from the root *ma*, "to measure, build, or form"; it is cognate to "magic," the production, whether by supernatural means or by mere camouflage, of an appearance that is in some way deceptive. When the Indians say the world is maya and we translate the word as illusion we should not take this to mean that the world does not exist at all, in any way or form. There is indeed a moon-larger-than-the-polestar, namely the one we see; we err only if we credit our perception with more objectivity than it deserves. Maya signals not that the world is unreal but that the way it presents itself to us is tricky. The carpet it unrolls before our feet and invites us onto is a magic carpet: it is enchanted—its fabric is in important part a fabrication. Maya is caveat, a warning, a call to alertness lest we be duped by the spell the world casts over us, whence the Buddha's insistence on "right mindfulness" and Islam's on *dhikr* or remembrance. "Life is the passage of an individual dream, a consciousness, an ego through a cosmic and collective dream. Death withdraws the particular dream from the general dream and tears out the roots which the former has sent down into the latter. The universe is a dream woven of dreams: the Self alone is awake."[4]

2. The Other-Than-the-Seeming Is a "More"; Indeed, a Stupendous More

Science and tradition agree, we see, in insisting that the way things really are is radically different from the way they seem. They also agree in claiming that this "other" than the way things appear lies in the direction of more rather than less. It outstrips anything everyday experience might suspect.

As science is essentially the domain of the quantifiable, the more that it has brought to light is registered primarily in

4. Frithjof Schuon, *Spiritual Perspectives and Human Facts* (London: Perennial Books, 1969), p. 169.

numbers.[5] We noted in the opening chapter of this book that it takes light from the closest sizable galaxy more than 2 million light-years to reach us, and the galaxies in the universe number in the billions. If we look in the opposite direction the figures are equally incomprehensible. Avogadro's number tells us that the molecules in $4\frac{1}{2}$ drams of water (roughly half an ounce) number 6.023×10^{23}—roughly 600,-000 billion billion.

To this more in the world's size that science reports tradition juxtaposes a qualitative more-than-we-normally-suppose. "I consider that the sufferings of this present time are not worth comparing with the glory that is to be revealed to us," Paul wrote to the Romans (8:18), while Gregory of Nyssa put the matter as follows:

> You are made in the likeness of that nature which surpasses all understanding. . . . Nothing in all creation can equal your grandeur. . . . If you realize this you will no longer marvel even at the heavens. . . . For the heavens pass away, but you will abide for all eternity with him who is forever.

The heading of this section suggested that the "more" to which science and tradition point, each in its own way, is not only more but stupendously more. The items that have been cited may already have made this case, but for the sake of the record it should be noted that they are only a beginning. Already by midcentury Fred Hoyle could say for science that "no literary imagination could have invented a story one-hundredth part as fantastic as the sober facts that have been unearthed,"[6] yet the quarter-century that has intervened has

5. Primarily but not exclusively. Along with its quantitative revelations science has discovered nature's elegance, too, to be beyond what had been supposed. "If there is one important result that comes out of our inquiry into the nature of the Universe it is this: when by patient inquiry we learn the answer to any problem, we always find, both as a whole and in detail, that the answer thus revealed is finer in concept and design than anything we could ever have arrived at by a random guess." Fred Hoyle, *The Nature of the Universe* (New York: New American Library, 1950), p. 128.

6. *Ibid.*, p. 120.

dwarfed even his purview. While microphysics probes for quarks that make the subatomic powers we have thus far named look immense, things 100 billion billion times smaller than the electron,[7] John Wheeler tells us that the entire universe we know—13 billion years old, 26 billion light-years across, filled with galaxies that too are now estimated to be in the billions—is but one of who knows how many likely trajectories of universes across a gigantic platform of superspace whose dimensions are not three or four but infinite. As for levels, though to enter even a single level of smallness beyond the one that is now being explored would require that we build an accelerator roughly the size of our planet, David Bohm thinks that the total number of levels in nature probably equals Wheeler's dimensions. They too are infinite.[8]

Quality cannot be precisely quantified, but it is interesting to note that when tradition uses numbers to *suggest* qualitative degrees it gives the astronomers a run for their money. Shankara gives us a notion of the extravagance of his vision of the *summum bonum* when he says that it "cannot be obtained except through the merits of 100 billion well-lived incarnations."[9] The Taittiriya Upanishad goes into the matter in greater detail.

> Let there be a noble young man who is well read [in the Vedas], very swift, firm, and strong, and let the whole world be full of wealth for him—that is one measure of human bliss.
> One hundred times that human bliss is one measure of the bliss of human gandharvas [demigods, the musicians of heaven], and

7. We now know that it was naïve to think that a "vacuum" is empty; it is populated, but by things that are utterly small. By the well-founded law that the shorter the wavelength the larger the energy that is compressed into it, we arrive at the conclusion that "in a thimbleful of vacuum there is more . . . energy than would be released by all the atomic bomb fuel in the universe." Quoted in Harold Schilling, *The New Consciousness in Science and Religion* (Philadelphia: United Church Press, 1973), p. 110.

8. The infinities of science are such, of course, only with respect to the categories in question, none of which comes close to being unlimited in all respects. Strictly speaking, there is only one Infinite, but that point is not at issue here.

9. *Crest-Jewel of Discrimination* (New York: New American Library, 1970), p. 35.

likewise of a great sage learned in the Vedas and free from desires.

One hundred times that bliss of the divine gandharvas is one measure of the bliss of the Fathers, enjoying their celestial life. . . .

One hundred times that bliss of the Fathers is one measure of the bliss of the devas [demigods] who are endowed with heavenly bodies through the merit of their lawful duties. . . .

One hundred times that bliss of the devas is one measure of the bliss of the devas who are endowed with heavenly bodies through the merit of the Vedic sacrifices. . . .

One hundred times that bliss of the sacrificial gods is one measure of the bliss of the thirty-three devas who live on the sacrificial offerings. . . .

One hundred times that bliss of the thirty-three devas is one measure of the bliss of Indra. . . .

One hundred times that bliss of Indra is one measure of the bliss of Brihaspati. . . .

One hundred times that bliss of Brihaspati is one measure of the bliss of Prajapati. . . .

One hundred times that bliss of Prajapati is one measure of the Bliss of Brahman [II. viii. 1–4],

for a total of one-followed-by-twenty-zeros times the bliss of the happiest worldling: 10^{19}.[10] As Atman, this supernal bliss resides obscured in each one of us. Typically, however, India does not bother with such number games, but moves right to the point. Like Wheeler's dimensions and Bohm's levels, Brahman's *ananda* (bliss) is infinite.

3. In Their Further Reaches the World's "Mores" Cannot Be Known in Ordinary Ways

What science shows, a physicist has recently observed, is that our view of things has no chance of being true unless it is

10. Cf. Chapter 11 of *The Diamond Sutra*: If galaxies equal in number to the square of the number of grains of sand in the Ganges River were to be filled with gold, silver, lapis-lazuli, crystal, agate, red pearls, and cornelian, the treasure thus amassed would be less by far than that derivable from four lines of *The Diamond Sutra*. Condensed from *Buddhist Wisdom Books*, trans. by Edward Conze (London: George Allen & Unwin Ltd., 1958), p. 49.

astonishing. But astonishment admits of degrees. With the exception of a footnote, the astonishing aspects of science we have thus far noted pertain to size and number. These already border on the incomprehensible—who can concretely imagine billions of billions?—but in the sequence of science's surrealistic uncoverings they are only the start. There comes a point where the nature science tracks turns a corner our minds cannot maneuver, leaving us, at that point, not astonished but astounded.

We have been treating science as basically the domain of the quantifiable and shall continue to do so—mathematics, we repeat, is its natural language—but this need not blind us to qualitative differences that do appear within it. The examples of these that are usually cited—the so-called secondary qualities of color, temperature, solidity/liquefaction, and the like that characterize the meso- but not the micro-world—are not the interesting ones here, for the *way* science deals with these continues to be spatio-temporal-quantitative. More interesting is the qualitative change that at a given point comes over science's epistemology, its knowing process.

The shift occurs when the physicist comes upon the very large and fast in nature, or conversely the very small; the former has spawned relativity theory, while the latter has required the invention of a new kind of mechanics especially designed for it, namely, quantum mechanics. Though these disciplines are occupied with opposite ends of the size continuum, they are partners in having worked man into a new epistemological situation.

It is customary to describe this situation by saying that nature in these reaches is "counterintuitive," meaning that it disregards and violates—transcends—the categories of space and time as we intuit them.

As human beings we live, as we have seen, in a middle kingdom; a meso-kingdom flanked by a micro-kingdom within and a macro-kingdom without. That our senses detect the meso-kingdom only—this too has been noted. The point now to be added is that the registers of nature that flank the one we directly encounter differ from ours not only in degree but in kind. On these outer registers nature behaves in ways that are passing strange. They are foreign to the point of being not merely unorthodox but downright scandalous. Put together two facts—(1) the fact that nature at its edges performs in ways that differ in kind from the way it meets our senses, and (2) the fact that our imaginations have nothing to build with save the building blocks our senses provide—and we arrive at the point the phrase "counterintuitive" was coined to make. In its further reaches the physical universe dons forms and functions we cannot visualize, in imagination any more than with the eyes in our heads. There is no way in which we can image them.

Light is the standard example, though actually the point concerns all matter. Is light wave or particle? Certain experiments show it to behave like one, others like the other. But waves and particles are different kinds of things. A particle is an entity like a stone; waves are like the ripples that spread from the stone's being dropped into a lake. To describe waves requires introducing the notion of movement (changes over periods of time)—otherwise we have only static ridges— whereas a stone can be described nontemporally. As we cannot visualize something that is simultaneously both rock and ripple, we would like to know which light really is. Hubris, the physicist snorts; must one know everything? If there is a something underlying wave and particle which light really is, it is a something for which our senses provide no analogue and which we can therefore never hope to image concretely. So with virtually everything in nature's recesses. In those never-never, through-the-looking-glass abodes, parallel lines meet, curves get you from star to star more quickly than do Euclid's straight lines, a particle will pass through alternative apertures simultaneously without dividing, time shrinks and expands, electrons (taking their cue from St. Thomas's angels who simply will themselves into different locations and find

themselves there) jump orbit without traversing the intervening distance, and particles fired in opposite directions, each at
a speed approximating that of light, separate from each other
no faster than the speed of light.

> The normal reaction to a first exposure to relativity is: "I think
> I understand it; I just don't believe it." Normally it takes a physi-
> cist about five years of contact with the ideas before he feels com-
> fortable with them—not because they are complex or obscure, but
> just terribly strange.
>
> The rule of the game is to *accept* the consequences of the postu-
> late no matter how weird. We must never ask *how* they can be so;
> we accept that they must be so, and see if any of the strange things
> they imply actually contradict our experience. The reader is im-
> plored to *have faith*, in the hope that all will turn out self-con-
> sistent in the end.[11]

One might put the matter this way: If modern science
showed that our senses are false witnesses, postmodern science
is showing that the human imagination is comparably defec-
tive.[12] It simply was not devised to reflect nature's total gamut.
For to repeat, imagination has no alternative but to build its
scenarios out of the photographic frames our senses provide,
which frames draw from only a tiny band in matter's varied
continuum. It was this that provoked Haldane's famous "mut-
terance" that "the universe is not only queerer than we
suppose, but queerer than we *can* suppose." David Finkel-
stein's sequel is that respecting nature "we haven't the capacity
to imagine anything crazy enough to stand a chance of being
right."

The limitations to which imagination is subject hold equally

11. Robert March, *Physics for Poets* (New York: McGraw-Hill, 1970),
p. 128.

12. "Contemporary physics [spells] the end of all hopes of interpreting
the . . . elements . . . of physical reality in sensory (visual-tactual) terms.
Human imagination is clearly incompetent to provide the material from
which a satisfactory model of matter can be built. . . . The possibility
of . . . pictorial . . . models of the transphenomenal level [is] forever
excluded." Milič Čapek, *Philosophical Impact of Contemporary Physics*
(Princeton: D. van Nostrand Co., 1961), pp. 398–99.

for language, for one step removed, it too derives from our sensed and workaday world. The distortions that result from trying to force nature into pictures of it—of a kind with those that occur when we try to chart our three-dimensional world on a two-dimensional Mercator map: Greenland always balloons absurdly—are mimed by the "howlers" that arise when we try to describe its distant regions in everyday speech. The polite word for the predicaments language leads to in these areas is "paradox," but the unvarnished fact is contradiction. "If we ask whether the electron's position changes with time," writes Robert Oppenheimer, "we must say 'No'; if we ask whether the position of the electron remains the same, we must say 'No'; if we ask whether the electron is at rest, we must say 'No'; if we ask whether it is in motion, we must say 'No.'"

On hearing a statement of this sort François Mauriac shook his head, remarking, "What this professor says is far more incredible than what we poor Christians believe." Actually, however, this is not so. We saw in the preceding section that the value claims of the traditions fully equal science's numerical claims; they climax in *ens perfectissimum*, perfect being, and perfection is the value equivalent of infinity. The parallelism continues as we now note that this value apex exceeds imagery[13] and ordinary discourse fully as much as do the data of quantum mechanics and relativity theory. The philosophical equivalent of "counterintuitive" is "ineffable" or "apophatic." At first, Dionysius the Areopagite tells us, the divine presence

is shown walking upon those heights of His holy places which are perceived by the mind; [but] then It breaks forth, even from those things that are beheld . . . and plunges the true initiate into the Darkness of Unknowing wherein he renounces all the apprehen-

13. "I do not admit at all that one who examines the realities by reasoning makes use of images," Plato observes in *Phaedo* (100A), having made clear that by "realities" he means things that reside at the upper end of the ontological continuum.

sions of his understanding and is wrapped in that which is wholly intangible and invisible.[14]

Ruysbroeck concurs:

> Enlightened men are . . . lifted above reason into a bare and imageless vision wherein lies the eternal indrawing summons of the Divine Unity; and with an imageless and bare understanding they . . . reach the summit of their spirits. There, their bare understanding is drenched through by the Eternal Brightness.[15]

The more we try to comprehend Perfection or even the heavens pictorially, the more credibility drains out of them, leaving us with cardboard cutouts of pearly gates and streets of gold, sloe-eyed houris or thousand-armed divinities. If, perceiving this, we retreat from visualization to abstract depictions, we find that propositions serve us no better than they did Oppenheimer. They land us in contradictions: "the wall of the Paradise in which Thou, Lord, dwellest is built of contradictories."[16] Notwithstanding the infinite difference between God and man, Christ is fully both. The persons of the Trinity are completely distinct *and* completely fused; they are fused but not confused, as the Creeds have it. Or the mystical experience. "We shall find," writes W. T. Stace,

> that paradoxicality is one of the common characteristics of all mysticism. . . . The assertion of this new kind of consciousness is completely paradoxical. One way of bringing out the paradox is to point out that what we are left with here, when the contents of consciousness are gone, is a kind of consciousness which has no objects. It is not a consciousness *of* anything, yet it is still consciousness. . . . Another aspect of the paradox is that this pure consciousness is simultaneously both positive and negative, something and nothing, a fullness and emptiness. It is pure peace, beatitude, joy . . . but . . . it is quite correct to say also that when

14. *The Divine Names and The Mystical Theology*, trans. by C. E. Rolt (London: S.P.C.K., 1971), p. 194.

15. Quoted in W. T. Stace, *The Teachings of the Mystics* (New York: New American Library, 1960), p. 62.

16. Nicholas of Cusa, *De Visione Dei*, Ch. IX, fin.

we empty out all objects and contents of the mind there is *nothing whatever left*. . . . The commonest metaphor for the positive side is light and for the negative side darkness. . . . We must not say that what we have here is a light *in* the darkness. For that would be no paradox. The paradox is that the light *is* the darkness, and the darkness *is* the light.[17]

If we should like to tighten to identity the similarity between such statements and Oppenheimer's, we can do so easily. "The depths of the Holy Spirit," the *Philokalia* tells us, "are not as the depths of the sea; they are the living waters of eternal life. The mind enters therein after relinquishing everything visible and mental [discursive] and *moves* and turns *motionlessly* among those incomprehensible things."[18] "He is both at rest and in motion, and yet is in neither state."[19]

4. The "Mores" That Cannot Be Known in Ordinary Ways Do, However, Admit of Being Known in Ways That Are Exceptional

From the point of view of ordinary language, the further reaches of both nature and spirit lie in the domain of the inexpressible. Or to put it the other way, they can be voiced only on pain of contradiction. It is as though, unable to say green, we were forced to say that a leaf is both yellow and blue while being neither.

But though the domains in question cannot be known by way of imagery and consistent description, they can be known in ways that are tailored to their exceptional referents. The epistemological device for discerning matter's farther reaches is mathematics: nature can no longer be consistently imaged or described in ordinary language, but it can be consistently

17. *Teachings of the Mystics*, pp. 16, 22–23.
18. E. Kadloubovsky and G. E. H. Palmer, *Writings from the Philokalia on the Prayer of the Heart* (London: Faber and Faber, 1951), p. 132 (italics added).
19. Dionysius the Areopagite, *The Divine Names and The Mystical Theology*, p. 143.

conceived through equations.[20] The comparably specialized way of knowing reality's highest transcorporeal reaches is the mystic vision.

The word "mystic" derives from the Greek root *mu*, meaning silent or mute—*muo* = "I shut my mouth"—and by derivation unutterable, which is the respect in which the word lends itself here. Called *satori* or *kensho* in the Ch'an (Zen) tradition, the vision broke over Hui-neng while he listened to a chanting of the Diamond Sutra, over Te-shan as he watched his master blow out a candle flame, over Ling-yun as he saw a blossom fall, over Hakuin on hearing a beat of his temple's gong, and over Po-chang when his master twisted his nose. Obviously the insight is not limited to Asia. The Lord appearing high and lifted up to Isaiah; the heavens opening to Christ at his baptism; the universe turning into a bouquet of flowers for Buddha beneath the bo tree; John reporting, "I was in the isle that is called Patmos . . . and . . . I was in the Spirit"; Saul struck blind on the Damascus road. . . . For St. Augustine it was the voice of a child saying, "Take, read"; for St. Francis a voice that seemed to come from the crucifix. It was while St. Ignatius sat by a stream and watched the running water, and Jakob Böhme was gazing at a pewter dish, that there came to each that news of another world which it is always religion's business to convey.

The message is always the same. Upon analysis we find that it consists of four components:

1. The first we have just been noting: the insight is *ineffable*. Emphatically it knows, but like higher mathematics, *what* it knows is so little contiguous with ordinary knowing that scarcely a hint of it can be conveyed to the uninitiated. On balance, therefore, we must say that it is incommunicable.

20. "Resolution . . . of the particle-wave paradox . . . was achieved . . . by the adoption of purely mathematical symbols (those of quantum mechanics) and, in general, by eschewing pictorially suggestive concepts wherever possible." Schilling, *The New Consciousness in Science and Religion*, pp. 78–79.

There are tribes along the Amazon that have no sugar. When anthropologists tried to describe to them the meaning of the word "sweet" the natives asked, "Is it like alligator meat?" Negotiation finally settled on human milk as the closest equivalent. We have already watched Dionysius call his quintessential knowing "Unknowing." Because the "mysteries of heavenly Truth lie hidden in the obscurity of the secret Silence, outshining all brilliance with the intensity of their darkness," he titles the opening chapter of his *Mystical Theology*, numinously, "The Divine Gloom."

2. The vision shows existence to be characterized by an entirely unexpected *unity*. Here we come upon another striking parallel with science, for its advance scouts too report things to be integrated beyond anticipation. Matter and energy are one. Time and space are one, time being space's fourth dimension. Space and gravity are one: the latter is simply space's curvature. And in the end matter and its space-time field are one: matter is "a local deformation of the spatio-temporal medium. More accurately, what was called a material body is nothing but a *center of this deformation*."[21] On the parallel track of the world's worth the mystic keeps step. He sees earth joined to heaven and man fused with God. "Hear, O Israel; the Lord our God, the Lord is *one*"; one in a sense that is all-embracing and all-reconciling. In the mystic vision at-one-ment is not a state to be achieved but a condition to be recognized, for God has united his divine essence with our inmost being. *Tat tvan asi*; That thou art. Atman *is* Brahman; samsara, Nirvana.

3. The discovery naturally awakens *joy*.

4. But it must be immediately added that the joy is not fortuitous. It is the logical consequence of the cause that preceded it: the discovery of being's unity. The point is crucial, for without it the mystic vision is demoted to mystical experience. The vision is, of course, an experience in the vacuous

---

21. Milič Čapek, *Philosophical Impact of Contemporary Physics*, p. 266.

sense that everything that comes man's way can be included in this loosest of all words. But by the same token, to call it an experience is to say nothing unless the point of the word is to stress its feeling tone. And this is precisely what must not be done on pain of debasing the currency. Feeling is a sentiment. To approach the mystic primarily on his feeling side is sentimental in the strict, pejorative sense toward which stress on the feeling aspect of things inevitably slopes. The mystic vision is not a feeling: it is a seeing, a knowing. We could add that it is a knowing that involves being—the man of God, says Eckhart, "is never rejoiced; he is joy itself"—but it is enough if we stop here with the fact that it is a knowing. It is *noetic*. In the words of William James, its disclosures afford "insight into depths of truth unplumbed by the discursive intellect. They are illuminations, revelations, full of significance and importance." Miss this point and there is no explanation for the fact that "they carry with them a curious sense of authority for aftertime."[22]

5. The Distinctive Ways of Knowing Which the Exceptional Regions of Reality Require Must Be Cultivated

Some regions of nature we experience directly, others we do not. But even these hidden regions can get messages to us in roundabout ways or we would not know that they exist. Had there been no lodestones on our planet we might still not know about magnetism, but lodestones do exist, and given that fact someone eventually picked up their signal.

Scanning for such signals and tracking their import is a demanding endeavor. It takes time to become a physicist today. The facts that relativity accounts for can be memorized in a few minutes, but years of study may not suffice to master the theory that places these facts in context. The dedication in science rivals that of saints and lovers; awakened it makes asceticism easy and natural. Was it Rutherford who, asked how

22. *The Varieties of Religious Experience* (New York: Collier Books, 1961), p. 300.

he discovered the composition of the radiation emitted by radioactive substances, replied, "I don't think I thought about another thing for seven years"?

At first glance it might seem that mystic knowing does not presuppose this kind of discipline and training, for its theophanies can arrive unsought and unprepared for. A Zen master has ventured that almost everyone at some time in his life experiences at least a light *kensho* (illumination), and the pages of Alcoholics Anonymous are replete with accounts of dissolutes to whom Heaven opened when their hope was gone. The difference between science and religion on this count is real, but we must distinguish on the religious side between individuals who experience flashes of insight and others who stabilize these flashes and turn them into abiding light. This stabilization need not require that the terrain the light discloses remain in direct view; William James lists transitoriness as a defining feature of the mystic state.[23] It is enough if the terrain is remembered, but the memory must be operative rather than idle—between the two lies literally a world of difference. Operatively remembered, the mystic's insight stabilizes to become his defining sense of reality. And thereupon it takes command—this is the "curious sense of authority for aftertime" that James found mystic insight to exercise. But for the mystic's vision to become definitive, things must be done—as many as the scientist must do in his arena. There is no point in raising here the issue of works versus grace, for though the emphasis can fall on one side or the other, there is no quest that does not include them both. Even in Zen it is grace that gives the student the determination to sit;[24] even in Shin the supplicant must himself pronounce the *nambutsu*.[25] Everything is a gift, but nothing is free. "The wind

23. *Ibid.*, p. 372. "Mystical states cannot be sustained for long. Except in rare instances, half an hour, or at most an hour or two, seems to be the limit beyond which they fade into the light of common day."

24. See Marco Pallis, "Is There Room for 'Grace' in Buddhism?" in Jacob Needleman, ed., *The Sword of Gnosis* (Baltimore: Penguin Books, 1974).

25. See Daisetz Suzuki, *Collected Writings on Shin Buddhism* (Kyoto: Shinshu Otaniha, 1973).

of God's grace is always blowing," Vivekananda used to say, "but you must raise your sail." "The knowledge of God cannot be attained by seeking, but only those who seek it find it" (Bayazid).

If the need for vigilance and endeavor (spiritual exercises) cuts across the free-will/grace divide, it likewise transcends the question of whether the training proceeds within the world or apart from it, in monasteries and deserts or through "the yoga of everyday life." Asked whether the spiritual quest requires asceticism, a Buddhist replied, "With the demands the world makes on us for patience, who needs contrived *askesis*?"

6. Profound Knowing Requires Instruments

Finally, in both science and religion frontier knowledge is disclosed only through the use of instruments. With the unaided eye a small, faint smudge can be detected in the constellation of Orion, and doubtless an imposing cosmological theory could be founded on this smudge. But no amount of theorizing, however ingenious, could ever tell us as much about the galactic and extragalactic nebulae as can direct acquaintance by means of a good telescope, camera, and spectroscope.

What are the mystic counterparts of such instruments? Basically they are two, one of which is corporate, the other private. For collectivities—tribes, societies, civilizations, traditions—the revealing instruments are the Revealed Texts, or, in nonliterate societies, the ordering myths that are impounded in stories. If one is put off by literalistic depictions of an anthropomorphic God who dictates these texts, he might provisionally think of the truths as welling up from the deepest unconscious of spiritual paragons, for, as we have seen, in the last resort Spirit (the divine in man) and the Infinite (the divine in its transpersonal finality) are identical—man's deepest unconscious is the mountain at the bottom of the lake. In either case, "in the beginning," that *illo tempore* of man's once-upon-a-time, there came to the Moseses and Muhammads of humanity the *shruti* (Truth that is heard) in comparison with which all subsequent truth is *smriti* (truth that is remembered).

These revealed canons are the "Palomar telescopes" that disclose the heavens that declare God's glory, but in this, religion's case, other more individual instruments are required as well. There comes a point when the mystic's instrument cannot stop with being external and must become—himself. All knowing involves an adequation of something in the knower to its object, but in the kind of knowing that is at issue here, this epistemological something cannot be limited to the knower's mind and senses. When Blake tells us that "if the doors of perception were cleansed every thing would appear to man as it is, infinite," the doors in question involve the total self. "It is a fact, confirmed and re-confirmed by two or three thousand years of religious history," Aldous Huxley wrote, "that Ultimate Reality is not clearly and immediately apprehended except by those who have made themselves loving, pure in heart, and poor in spirit." These are the tools for facilitating the mystic's key perceptions that solve all riddles at a stroke and define reality from that point on.

According to the Sufis, the verses of the Koran contain a minimum of seven and a maximum of seventy hidden, symbolic significances. By this reckoning we are one short, having listed only six ways in which science serves as symbol, illuminating through parallels man's spiritual thrust. Were we to add a seventh, it would be this: Beginning with the corporeal plane as its object, science comes at length on strata where the spacio-temporal-material matrices of that plane grow at first spongy and then fade out entirely. A summary of the position of Paul Dirac, the father of antimatter, on this point reads as follows:

All matter is created out of some imperceptible substratum and . . . the creation of matter leaves behind it a "hole" in this substratum which appears as antimatter. Now, this substratum itself is not accurately described as material, since it uniformly fills all space and is undetectable by any observation. In a sense, it appears as nothingness—immaterial, undetectable, and omnipresent. But it is a peculiarly material form of nothingness, out of which all matter is created.[26]

In parallel vein John Wheeler, father of superspace, the quintessence of relativity, writes:

A . . . drastic conclusion emerges out of quantum geometrodynamics and displays itself before our eyes in the machinery of superspace: *there is no such thing as spacetime in the real world of quantum physics.* . . .

On this picture physics is a staircase. Each tread registers a law. . . . Each riser marks the transcendence of that law. . . . The staircase climbs from step to step: density, and density found alterable; valence law, and valence law melted away: conservation of net baryon and net lepton number, and these conservation laws transcended; conservation of energy and angular momentum, and these laws likewise overstepped; and then the top thread displaying all the key constants and basic dynamic laws—but above a final riser leading upward into nothingness. It bears a message: With the collapse of the universe, the framework falls down for every law of physics. There is no dynamic principle that does not require space and time for its formulation; but space and time collapse; and with their collapse every known dynamic principle collapses.[27]

Invoking the levels of reality that were outlined in Chapter 3, we say that science here bumps the ceiling of the corporeal plane. It can glimpse a land across the river, but its methods do not enable it to enter that land. From the metaphysical point of view its arms, lifted toward a zone of freedom that transcends coagulation, form the homing arc of the "love loop" noted on page 84. They are science responding to Eternity's love for the productions of time.

It is a far cry from antimatter and superspace to the mind of an aborigine, yet it is conceivable that if the whole sweep of science were to be spread before the latter he might see it in

26. Richard F. Plzak, Jr., "Paradox East and West," unpublished senior dissertation, M.I.T., 1973, p. 54.

27. "From Relativity to Mutability," in Jagdish Mehra (ed.), *The Physicist's Conception of Nature* (Dordrecht-Holland/Boston–U.S.A.: D. Reidel Publishing Company, 1973), pp. 227, 241.

better perspective than we do. In the opening pages of *The Savage Mind*, Lévi-Strauss quotes a native thinker as making a penetrating comment, the one we used as epigraph for this chapter: " 'All sacred things must have their place.' It could even be said," Lévi-Strauss continues,

> that being in their place is what makes them sacred for if they were taken out of their place, even in thought, the entire order of the universe would be destroyed. Sacred objects therefore contribute to the maintenance of the order of the universe by occupying the places allocated to them.[28]

So it is with science. In place it is a grace. Cyril Smith reminds us that metals and glass were invented for art and religion rather than utility, but technology bestows utilitarian favors as well, and science in addition to its intrinsic disclosures of truth can inspire awe and serve as a symbol to confirm the spirit's quest.[29] This last is the way we have tried to put it to work in this chapter: if there are sermons in stones it is inconceivable that none exist in science; in Latin "laboratory" (labor-oratory) means a place to work and pray. The converse of the foregoing is that out of place, as angel that has fallen, science turns demonic. It presumes to control too much and to disclose more of reality than in fact it does. To approach existence as if it were purely or even primarily physical and mathematical is to falsify it. The approach could end in smashing our planet, for if a hammer is the only tool one learns to use, it is tempting to regard everything as if it were a nail.

But we were not going to get involved in consequences.

28. Chicago: The University of Chicago Press, 1966, p. 10. Our language retains the memory of this early insight. The sublime is what remains within its limit—*sub-limen*.

29. Approaching physics from this angle, Fritjof Capra calls it "a path with a heart." *The Tao of Physics* (Berkeley: Shambala, 1975), p. 25.

> I no longer desired a better world, because I
> was thinking of creation as a whole: and in the
> light of this more balanced discernment, I had
> come to see that higher things are better than
> the lower, but that the sum of all creation is
> better than the higher things alone.
>
> ST. AUGUSTINE, *Confessions*, VII, xiii, 19

> I only pass on to others what [has been] passed
> on to me. If there is any lack of learning in my
> writing, any obscurity of expression or superficial
> treatment, you may feel sure that it is in such
> places that I am most original.
>
> ST. BELLARMINE

6. HOPE, YES; PROGRESS, NO

Hope is indispensable to human health—to psychological
health most immediately, but because man is a psychosomatic
whole, to physical health as well. Situated as we are in the
Middle (hence middling) World, vicissitudes are a part of the
human lot: external vicissitudes (hard times), and internal vicissitudes—the "gravitational collapse" of the psyche that sucks
us into depression as if it were a black hole. Against such vicissitudes hope is our prime recourse. Ascending a sheer-faced
cliff, a mountaineer can lodge his pick in an overhead crevice
and, chinning himself on it, advance. Hope is the psyche's
pick.

In the primordial outlook hope is vertical, or at least trans-
historical. "Vertical" here means that the fundamental change
that is hoped for is an ascent of the individual soul through a
medium—the world—which does not itself change substantially
but provides stable rungs on which the soul can climb. Or in
cases where the prospect is viewed collectively and in worldly
terms—as in the Kingdom of God that is to come "on earth,"
the coming age of the Maitreya Buddha, or Islam's Day of Res-

urrection—it is assumed that this Kingdom will differ in kind from the history that preceded it and will be inaugurated by God's direct if not apocalyptic intervention. In neither its individual nor its collective version is progress in the traditional sense envisioned as sociopolitical, the gradual amelioration of man's corporate lot through his collective efforts and ingenuity.

By contrast, the modern version of hope is emphatically historical. And its imagery is horizontal, for its eye is on an earthly future instead of the heavens. In one sense all hope is future-oriented, but that of modernity is doubly so—for mankind as a whole as well as for the individual. In fact, hope for individuals is for the most part tied to hope for history; it is on the hope that human life as a whole can be improved that hope for the individual primarily relies. If the traditional view rested its case on the fact that in boiling water bubbles rise, the modern view hopes to escalate the water itself.

What effected this Copernican revolution in the way hope —or progress; the same thing—is conceived? Three agents.

The first was science. Around the seventeenth century the scientific method began garnering information at an exponential rate. True, its findings pertained to physical nature only, but even so, the vista was breath-taking. Moreover, by virtue of improvements that occurred in methods of experimentation, the new understanding of nature could be *proved* to be true. It seemed evident, therefore, that in this one respect at least, corporate progress was being effected. Never again would mankind be as naïve as it has been regarding its habitat.

On the heels of this progress in pure understanding came science's utilitarian spin-off, technology. It multiplied goods, relieved drudgery, and counteracted disease. Since these are not inconsiderable benefactions and, like the findings of pure science, can be dispensed—bestowed on people, unlike character, say, which each individual must acquire for himself—it again looked as if mankind as a whole was advancing. History was getting somewhere.

These two causes for the rise of the vision of historical progress are well known. The third reason has been less noticed because it is privative; it involved not the appearing but the vanishing of something. Science and technology would not have changed man's outlook a fraction as much as they did had they not been reinforced by scientism. Its epistemological assumption that only the scientific method gives "news about the universe" produced the ontological conclusion that corporeal reality is the only concrete and self-sufficient reality there is; see Chapter 1. In a single stroke the mansion of being was reduced to its ground floor. The consequence for hope was obvious: if being has no upper stories, hope has no vertical prospect. If it is to go anywhere—and hope by definition implies a going of some sort—henceforth that "where" could only be forward or horizontal. The extent to which the modern doctrine of progress is the child, not of evidence as it would like to believe, but of hope's élan—the fact that being indispensable it *does* spring eternal in the human breast and, in the modern world view, has no direction to flow save forward —is among the undernoted facts of intellectual history. If the ratio between evidence and hope in the idea of historical progress were to be laid squarely before us, we would be humbled in our estimate of ourselves as rational creatures.

As things stand, we do not see that picture clearly and historical progress remains the kingpin of the modern outlook. Seeping and soaking, permeating, probing, it diffuses like mist, discovering every corner, saturating every cell. In biology we have Darwinism and evolution, in cosmology an evolving universe. In history we have *The Idea of Progress* (J. B. Bury) and Marx's escalator that rises from slavery and serfdom through capitalism to the coming classless society. In philosophy we have Henri Bergson's early-century *Creative Evolution* and Ernst Bloch's midcentury *Das Prinzip Hoffnung*, and in theology Jürgen Moltmann's Protestant *Theology of Hope* and the Catholic writings of Johannes Metz. Cutting across the lot, as if to pull the vision together, is the work of the scientist, poet, and mystic Teilhard de Chardin, as focused in *The Phenomenon of Man*.

Somewhere in his ponderous *All and Everything* Gurdjieff says in effect, "Now I am going to tell you something people are not going to believe." The statement galvanized our attention, for it seemed to us that the author had been trafficking in notions of this genre for some pages. With an interest the book had not up to then aroused, we raced to discover what this truly incredible truth was to be. It appeared that it would have to do with the reason for wars, and this looked promising; it would be very good, we thought, to know why human beings decimate their kind. We were not prepared for the answer. The reason for wars, it turns out, is that the moon feeds on human beings. Periodically its fare grows slim and a war is needed to beef it up. We thought: the man is right—absolutely, completely, unequivocally right. This people won't believe.

We relate this incident because we sense that it may be about to be reenacted with its roles reversed. Readers who feel that the notions of the last several chapters have already pressed credulity to the limit—notions like the survival of bodily death, incorporeal realms that are more real than physical ones, or infinite beatitude as the human possibility—may find the point we are about to make, the last major one of this work, excessive; *de trop*, as the French would say: too much. In traditional China a gentleman might be found protesting that a friend's modesty "exceeds the permitted limits." Readers may feel that what we are about to say likewise exceeds limits; the limits of credulity most obviously, but possibly of propriety as well. For we are going to say that progress is an illusion; not only future progress but past progress as well. The last part of that statement will have to be qualified, but in essence it will stand. Utopia is a dream, evolution a myth.

To refer to the illusion in its total sweep, we coin the word "prevolution." Phonetically the word joins *pro*gress to *evolution*, showing the two to be faces, prospective and retrospective, of a single, Janus-like deity. In addition the word suggests the current *prevalence* of the cult of this god. The impounding of these ideas in a single word gives us a running start into our theme.

If Western man were to see that this god is a false one—or to put it the other way, that prevolution is a fiction; it *has* not happened and *will* not happen—the modern age would be over, for the notion is so much its cornerstone that were it to crumble, a new edifice would have to be built. By the same token, the case against the notion is going to be difficult to make, for it is not easy to dislodge a notion that undergirds an entire epoch. We shall take it in segments. Working our way backward, we shall look successively at the long-range future, the short-range future, the short-range past, and the long-range past.

The long-range prospects for our universe are not encouraging. Whether it ends by collapsing into a widening black hole[1] or winds down to an entropic deep freeze four degrees above absolute zero does not much matter; be the finale a bang or a whimper, its human import is the same: our universe will not support life indefinitely.[2] Given the rate at which the sun is

1. "The black hole of today is more than a black hole. It is a symbol, 'experimental model,' and provider of lessons for the collapse Einstein predicted in far later days for the universe itself." John Wheeler, in Jagdish Mehra (ed.), *The Physicist's Conception of Nature* (Dordrecht-Holland/Boston–U.S.A.: D. Reidel Publishing Company, 1973), p. 215.

2. I insert a footnote which is at least interesting; whether it is more than that the reader may decide for himself. When in 1964 I had my first audience with His Holiness the Dalai Lama, I resolved in advance not to take much of his valuable time and after about ten minutes arose to take my leave. He stood up with me, and though we had been conversing through an interpreter I heard him say to himself in English, "I must decide what is important." There was a moment's pause, then a smile broke over his face and with the words "Please be seated," he gestured to the divan. When I next arose an hour and three-quarters had elapsed for the most remarkable morning of my life.

What secured for me this gift was not, it turned out, good karma but rather a ruse. In Asia calling cards are useful, and the one I had sent ahead in requesting the audience carried in its lower left-hand corner the words "Massachusetts Institute of Technology." It proved to be a magic name, for along with his sanctity and erudition, His Holiness has a lively scientific interest and a mechanical bent: he strips down Austin Healeys and dismantles watches to reassemble them. My card had misled him into

spending its energy, our particular solar system will die long before our universe does, of course. In 5 billion years it will have thinned out to 250 times its present diameter and swallowed our planet.

Such prospects caused a former dean of Canterbury Cathedral to cry, "Short views, for God's sake, short views." But with the

thinking that he had a flesh-and-blood scientist in his living room, and he had decided not to pass up the opportunity this afforded.

Specifically, he wanted to check two scientific reports that had recently come his way. One of these concerned DNA; he wanted to know if it bore at all on the doctrine of reincarnation. The other concerned cosmogonies. He had heard of Hoyle's steady-state theory in which a continuing influx of hydrogen (from who knows where) compensates for the thinning out of matter through the world's expansion, and also of the so-called big-bang theory which posits that at its start our universe consisted of a superdense kernel that exploded and has been expanding ever since. To these I was able to add a third, which Harlow Shapley called the bang-bang-bang theory: the theory that the present expanding phase of our universe will be followed by one of collapse, with no reason why the cycle should not repeat itself, accordion fashion, indefinitely. His Holiness nodded, saying that of the three this last was the most nearly right. It has been interesting to note that in the decade since he registered that opinion the steady-state theory has been retired from the running. One waits with interest to see which of the other two receives the astronomers' imprimatur.

To insert brackets within parentheses, I cannot refrain from adding another point which strictly speaking has nothing to do with the topic under discussion but which mention of the Dalai Lama invariably brings to mind. No one I know who has been in his presence has failed to be impressed, least of all myself. But the way he impressed me was almost the reverse of my expectations, insofar as I recall having had any. For it was not as if he wore a halo or exuded some sort of numinous glow. Almost the opposite: from the moment he clasped my hand with a firmness that made it feel in comparison to his like a flabby fish, it was his directness, his utter unpretentiousness, his total objectivity, that astonished. I do not believe that before or since I have been in the presence of someone who was as completely himself. Because I have traveled considerably in "the mystical East" I am frequently asked if I have ever encountered the siddhis, the supernatural powers that are believed to accrue in the course of yogic training and advance. My answer is no, not directly. I have heard innumerable accounts from persons who claimed to have been firsthand witnesses, but always the displays have stopped one step short of my door. Since meeting the Dalai Lama, however, I sometimes add an appendage to that answer. How anyone could have been raised as that man was, like a queen bee, really, surrounded from the age of four by no one save persons who assumed as a matter of course that he was God-incarnate for Tibet—how, to repeat, a mortal could have survived this kind of upbringing and escaped the slightest trace of a big head is, I am inclined to think, as close to a miracle as I need come.

ecological crisis, energy depletion, the population explosion, and the proliferation of nuclear weapons, to say nothing of the interlocking, depersonalized bureaucratization of life,[3] the short-range future, too, looks bleak. Systems analysts, synthesizing their computer data, tell us we are on a collision course with disaster; Robert Heilbroner's *The Human Prospect* is not pleasant reading. Poets and philosophers had anticipated their warning. The century in which politicians have preyed on hope unprecedentedly, promising "The Century of the Common Man," "The War to End All Wars," "The War to Make the World Safe for Democracy," "The Four Freedoms," "The Great Society"—this century of maniacally inflated expectations has seen utopian writing come to a dead stop.[4] "Hope," Kazantzakis concluded, "is a rotten-thighed whore." Even Bergson, who moved Darwin into philosophy, came at the end to the view that man was "being crushed by the immense progress" he has made. Sartre is not profound, but he is a shrewd phenomenologist, and on the existential level where he works he advises that "we must learn to live without hope." The morning newspaper lists a film that is showing at a local cinema. Titled *I Have Seen the Future and It Doesn't Work*, it is billed for "mature" audiences.

But if the future will not work, surely the past has. Is not progress up to the present—life beginning in slime and ending in intelligence—a matter of record?

Let us see.

We begin with the short-range past, the career of *Homo sapiens* himself. To the prevolutionist, its career replicates the incline plane of the grand design: the species begins with ape men and moves through primitive savages to culminate in the intelligent creatures we have now become. The view is so taken for granted that when we hear the director of a leading

3. Ninety percent of the gainfully employed in the United States now work in organizations. Seventy years ago 90 percent were self-employed.

4. *Walden Two* is no exception to this statement. Its unconvincingness, stemming from its lack of insight more than its lack of artistry, debars it from serious consideration.

museum observe, "From Stone Age to the present—what a decline," we suspect him either of quipping or of fronting for a museum's vested interest in the past. Perhaps the discovery that the Neanderthal's brain was larger than ours will help us to take the judgment more seriously.[5] Or the assessment of Lévi-Strauss; in terms of man-nature equilibrium, which in the long run must be the ruling consideration, he places the Golden Age of humanity somewhere around the Neolithic.[6] If we shift from ecological to intellectual criteria, he again sees no clear advance; in a way the burden of his entire work has been to make clear that "the savage mind" is fully as complex and rational as our own. And if we go with him a final step, looking beyond rationality to the motives that determine its use, Lévi-Strauss sees decline. Is it that analytic thought (the kind man has fallen into) has unseen violence built into it? he asks; or that man is possessed by an obscure fury against the Eden he dimly remembers and unconsciously realizes that he has lost?

5. See Phillip V. Tobias, *The Brain in Hominid Evolution* (New York: Columbia University Press, 1971), pp. 96, 100–103. I am indebted to Gary Snyder, who is an anthropologist as well as a poet, for this point as well as the one in the next footnote.

6. Marshall Sahlins places it even earlier, in the Paleolithic; the view that the transition from hunting and gathering to agriculture constitutes a Great Leap Forward, he discounts as nothing but a "neolithic prejudice." Countering the entrenched theoretical position today, wherein the question "How did the primitives manage to live?" is topped only by the question of whether their existence deserves to be called living at all, he argues in his *Stone Age Economics* (Chicago and New York: Aldine-Atherton, Inc., 1972) that theirs was, as the title of his opening chapter puts it, "The Original Affluent Society." Affluence being a ratio between means and ends, by keeping their ends modest—want not, lack not—their means were more adequate to them than is the case with us. It is we who sentence ourselves to life at hard labor; the primitive is in business for his health. Hunters keep banking hours: "reports on hunters and gatherers . . . suggest a mean of three to five hours per adult worker per day in food production" (p. 34). The rest of their time is reserved for gossiping, entertaining, dancing and other arts, and daytime sleep. "Savage . . . days are nothing but a pastime," a seventeenth-century explorer reported (p. 29). Passing to the question of what our industry has got *us*, Sahlins answers: "*This* is the era of hunger unprecedented. Now, in the time of the greatest technical power, is starvation an institution. Reverse another venerable formula: the amount of hunger increases relatively and absolutely with the evolution of culture" (p. 26).

Whatever the reason, whenever man now comes on landscapes or communities that resemble his image of a lost innocence, he lashes out and lays waste. Colonizers, rapacious white men and their technology, are the conspicuous culprits, but Lévi-Strauss does not exempt himself and his own discipline. The Western hunt for knowledge, analytic and objective to its core, has violence built into it. For to know analytically is to reduce the object of knowledge, however vital, however complex, to precisely this: an object. This being so, the Western hunt for knowledge, anthropology not excepted, is in a tragic sense the final exploitation and, as George Steiner has observed, *Tristes Tropiques* the first classic of our current ecological anguish.

> It looks forward with haughty melancholy to the image of the globe—cooling, emptied of man, cleansed of his garbage—that appears in the coda of *Mythologiques*. "Anthropology," says Lévi-Strauss in concluding *Tristes Tropiques*, can now be seen as "entropology": the study of man has become the study of disintegration and certain extinction. There is no darker pun in modern literature.[7]

Extending our retrospective look past man to the story of life as a whole, we come to evolution in its classic, Darwinian sense. This is the key domain, for it is on biological evolution that prevolution finally builds; this is its bedrock and prime foundation. As biologist Lewis Thomas puts it, "Evolution is our most powerful story, equivalent in its way to a universal myth."

In his *Personal Knowledge*—a book once commended to us by Noam Chomsky as the best on the philosophy of science that has been written—Michael Polanyi opens his critique of Neo-Darwinism with this arresting remark: "Only a prejudice backed by genius can have obscured such elementary facts [contradicting this school] as I propose to state."[8] There is not space here to reproduce the details of his argument; we must

7. *The New Yorker*, June 4, 1974, pp. 107–108.
8. Chicago: University of Chicago Press, 1958, p. 382. Page references in the following paragraphs are to this work.

be content to summarize it. The history of nature shows "a cumulative trend of changes tending towards higher levels of organization, among which the deepening of sentience and the rise of thought are the most conspicuous" (p. 384). "At each successive stage of this epic process we see arising some novel operations not specifiable in terms of the preceding level" (p. 389); for example, "while quantum mechanics can explain in principle all chemical reactions, it cannot replace, even in principle, our knowledge of chemistry" (p. 384). The same holds, of course, for the relation of biology to chemistry, psychology to biology, and so on. Moreover,

the consecutive steps of a long-range evolutionary progress—like the rise of consciousness—cannot be determined *merely by their adaptive advantage*, since these advantages can form part of such progress only in so far as they prove adaptive in a *peculiar way, namely on the lines of continuous ascending evolutionary achievement*. The action of the ordering principle underlying such a persistent creative trend is necessarily overlooked or denied by the theory of natural selection. . . . Recognition [of this ordering principle] would. . . . reduce mutation and selection to their proper status of merely *releasing and sustaining the action of evolutionary principles* by which all major evolutionary achievements are defined. [p. 385]

The rise of man can be accounted for only by other principles than those known today to physics and chemistry. If this be vitalism, then vitalism is mere common sense, which can be ignored only by a truculently bigoted mechanistic outlook. And so long as we can form no idea of the way a material system may become a conscious, responsible person, it is an empty pretense to suggest that we have an explanation for the descent of man. Darwinism has diverted attention for a century from the descent of man by investigating the *conditions* of evolution and overlooking its *action*. Evolution can be understood only as a feat of emergence. [p. 390]

This last word, "emergence," epitomizes Polanyi's alternative to Darwinism and links him to the precursors he acknowledges, Lloyd Morgan and Samuel Alexander. The entire thrust of Polanyi's philosophical work is against reductionism, the attempt to explain the higher in terms of the lower, the whole in terms of its parts. In this, its negative polemic, it is on sure ground; the question concerns his alternative. Emergence is well and good, but where from? From whence do the "ordering innovative principles" he insists on (p. 387, *passim*) derive? If simpler, antecedent principles cannot account for them, is "nothing"—thin air—a more plausible source? For respecting sources, "nothing" and "thin air" are what emergence comes to. "All we can say is that at one moment there is nothing and at the next something," said Hoyle in answer to the question of where the hydrogen in his steady-state theory derived from. As etiology, emergence says no more than this.

Can anything come from nothing? Can a stream rise higher than its source? We are back to the enduring imponderables. On issues this fundamental, this close to ontological sensibility at its root and essence, no argument can deliver verdicts, so we shall enter none. Instead, we shall describe; we shall state. If emergence denies that a stream can rise higher than its source in the sense of simpler ordering principles accounting for ones that are more complex, the primordial outlook agrees with this denial and adds that something cannot come from nothing. *Ex nihilo nihil fit.*

What does this portend for evolution? It does not counter the fact that in the temporal order simple precedes complex. First viruslike specks of living matter; then bacilli with physiological functions that serve survival; then protozoa that can move about of their own accord and effect purposive activities; then multicellular organisms with sexual reproduction, nervous systems of increasing complexity, and sense organs that extend contact deeper into the surrounding space. We do not know when consciousness entered the sequence, but thought proper seems to come with the language that is confined to man. There is no need to deny anything in the sequence that carbon dating tells us transpired. Genesis had already announced the principle, as had other sacred texts and commentaries on them. "Man," said Gregory Palamas,

> this greater world contained in a lesser, [is] the concentration into one whole of all that is, the recapitulation of all things created by God. Therefore he was produced last of all, just as we also (in our turn) round off what we have to say with a conclusion.[9]

Far from denying life's progression, tradition provides a reason for it (in its own order of explanation, of course). Microcosm mirrors macrocosm, earth mirrors heaven. But mirrors, as we have noted, invert. The consequence here is that that which is first in the ontological order appears last in the temporal order.

Not that the higher appears after the lower but that it is produced by the lower—this is what tradition denies. In doing so it counters the dominant mood of our time. Order from revolution (Marx), ego from id (Freud), life from the primal ooze (Darwin); everywhere the reflexive impulse is to derive the more from the less. Tradition proceeds otherwise.

What difference does it make which way we proceed— whether we look up or down for our explanations? We feel enjoined to raise this question explicitly, for we fear the reader may at this point be experiencing a letdown. Taking off from Gurdjieff's "this they won't believe," we had more than intimated that on the question of life's origin we proposed to say something startling. The exotic expectations this introit may have conjured in the reader's mind can only be surmised. That man arrived from another planet? That he was molded directly from dust? And after this buildup the promised surprise turns out to be scarcely one at all. The evolutionary sequence is not denied: amoebas did come first; life does advance. The only difference attaches to what would seem to be a secondary issue: the means by which the advance is effected. In

9. *The Ascetic and Theological Teaching of Gregory Palamas,* trans. by Father Basil Krivosheine; reprint from *The Eastern Churches Quarterly,* No. 4, 1938, p. 3.

all other respects the prevailing view is ratified and what was billed as a shock wave turns out to be a ripple. Life does evolve.

No, it does not. The point at stake is not a detail or in any way secondary. For evolution does not present itself as mere chronicle, a timetable, so to speak, with curators lining up fossil remains in the sequences in which they appeared. Evolution proposes to be an explanatory theory. It is the claim that everything about man, his complete complement of faculties and potentials, can be accounted for by a process, natural selection, that works mechanically on chance variations. Let its most distinguished recent spokesman phrase the wording. "Evolution . . . the product of an enormous lottery presided over by natural selection, blindly picking the rare winners from among numbers drawn at utter random. . . . This conception alone is compatible with the facts. The miracle stands 'explained.' "[10]

The quotation marks around that last word are interesting, standing as they do as an acknowledgment that Monod himself recognizes that he is using the word "explained" atypically. He does not tell us the deviant sense he has in mind, but by our lights his departure from normal usage is major. For to someone not already predisposed in evolution's favor, *Monod's* "explanation" is not such at all.[11] One reads his book, takes a sounding of the evolutionary corpus, and the miracle remains.

Let us take our bearings. Why in a chapter on hope are we devoting so much space to evolution?

Because it bears decisively on the chapter's theme. We have saved hope for this last substantive chapter of the book, not only because of its importance to human well-being but because we see it as the topic on which current thought is most confused and mistaken. The mistake lies in founding hope on

10. Jacques Monod, *Chance and Necessity* (New York: Vintage Books, 1972), p. 138.
11. See William Pollard's telling critique of it in *Soundings*, LVI, 4 (Winter 1973). Also John Lewis (ed.), *Beyond Chance and Necessity* (Atlantic Highlands, N.J.: Humanities Press, 1974).

a collective future, a future that will upgrade the quality of life by the mere fact that lives are born into it. Of the two factors that gave rise to this error, the first—a blend of science and technology—we are on our way to seeing through. There remains its other prop: evolution. We have called it the king-pin of the modern mind because from the standpoint of that mind so much has come to rest on it—nothing less than hope itself—that modernity is more invested in this doctrine than in any other. This in itself should put us on alert respecting it, given what we know about the way desire vectors evidence in favor of its wishes.

To speak plainly, as long as we can believe that there is a principle operative in nature—natural selection—that works to produce the higher from the lower, we can take courage. God is reinstated; a different god to be sure, but akin to the earlier one in that "he" too will see to it that things turn out all right. He does not preclude false starts any more than his predecessor did, but in the long run the victory is assured. We are in good hands.

As a matter of fact that last sentence happens to be true—the title of this chapter implies as much. But the hands in question are not those of natural selection. Fortunately, con-sidering the latter's brittleness.

This is not the place to enter into a full-scale critique of the theory of evolution. Those who wish to pursue the subject will find the main points summarized in Section IV of Titus Burckhardt's remarkable essay "Cosmology and Modern Science"[12] and spelled out in considerable detail in Douglas Dewar's *The Transformist Illusion*[13] and Evan Shute's *Flaws*

12. In Jacob Needleman, ed., *The Sword of Gnosis* (Baltimore: Penguin Books, 1974).

13. Murfreesboro, Tenn.: De Hoff Publications, 1957. It shows, among other things, that the so-called missing links are still missing. The most commonly cited example in favor of the evolutionary hypothesis is the supposed genealogy of the equine animals, which Charles Deperet criticizes as follows: "Geological observation establishes in a formal manner that no gradual passage existed between these genera; the last *Palaeotherium* was extinct long since, without transforming itself, when the first *Archi-*

in the Theory of Evolution.[14] Regarding the empirical evidence we shall content ourselves with three things: our own summary assessment, the assessment of a biologist, and a prediction.

Our personal assessment is that on no other scientific theory does the modern mind rest so much confidence on so little proportional evidence; on evidence, that is to say, which, in ratio to the amount that would be needed to establish the theory in the absence of the will to believe, is so meager. In its standard form the evolutionary hypothesis lies too close to accepted belief for today's Westerner to see how much it rides the will to believe, but when the hypothesis is enlarged—blown up, as it were, like a photographic print—the "will" shows up in clear outline. Teilhard de Chardin provides the

---

therium appeared, and the latter had disappeared in its turn, without modification, before being suddenly replaced by the invasion of *Hipparion.* . . . The supposed pedigree of the *Equidae* is a deceitful delusion, which simply gives us the general process by which the tridactyl hoof of an Ungulate can transform itself, in various groups, into a monodactyl hoof, in view of an adaptation for speed; but in no way enlightens us on the palaeontological origin of the horse." *Le Transformations du Monde Animal,* pp. 107, 105; cited by Burckhardt on p. 144 and Dewar on p. 92.

Because the names of these authors are not household words, we add a summary statement by Loren Eiseley, whose name will be recognized: "How the primeval human creature evolved into *Homo sapiens,* what forces precipitated the enormous expansion of the human brain—these problems ironically still baffle the creature who has learned to weigh stars and to tamper with the very fabric of the universe." "Fossil Man," in *Scientific American,* CLXXXIX (Dec. 1953), 65. A final verdict in this list that could go on for pages comes from a former colleague at the Massachusetts Institute of Technology, Murray Eden: "Neo-Darwinian evolutionary theory . . . has been modified to the point that virtually every formulation of the principles of evolution is a tautology." "Inadequacies of Neo-Darwinian Evolution as a Scientific Theory," in Paul Moorhead and Martin Kaplan, eds., *Mathematical Challenges to the Neo-Darwinian Interpretation of Evolution* (Philadelphia: The Wistar Institute Press, 1967), p. 109. "Natural selection" has proved to be a key that can be twisted to fit almost any lock.

14. Nutley, N.J.: Craig Press, 1961. The contribution of this book lies in the clear distinction it draws between "micro-evolution" (evolution on a small scale and within narrow limits), which no one contests, and "mega-evolution" (the theory that the class of birds, for example, evolved from the class of reptiles), which is "really a philosophy dating from the days of biological ignorance; it was a philosophical synthesis built up in a biological kindergarten."

obvious instance. To him, *The Phenomenon of Man* was science, a clean print-out—"pure and simple" are his words—of the conclusions the facts of nature point to. P. B. Medawar is as schooled in those facts as Teilhard was, but since he does not approach them by way of Teilhard's pseudo-Christian assumptions, he does not find them pointing to the Omega Point at all. The greater part of Teilhard's argument, Medawar writes,

> is nonsense, tricked out by a variety of tedious metaphysical conceits, and its author can be excused of dishonesty only on the grounds that before deceiving others he has taken great pains to deceive himself. *The Phenomenon of Man* cannot be read without a feeling of suffocation, a gasping and flailing around for sense. There is an argument in it, to be sure—a feeble argument, abominably expressed—but . . . it is the style that creates the illusion of content, and which is in some part the cause as well as merely the symptom of Teilhard's alarming apocalyptic seizures.[15]

Touché! And *pari passu!* Our point is that if biologists were to approach the paleontological record as innocent of evolutionary biases as Medawar is unencumbered by Teilhardian ones, their frustration in the face of the claimed scientific status of the evolutionary theory would rival Medawar's frustration on reading the assertion with which *The Phenomenon of Man* opens and on which the book turns; the assertion that "this book . . . must be read not as a work on metaphysics, still less as a sort of theological essay, but purely and simply as a scientific treatise."

As our judgment here is open to the double charge that not only is it that of a layman but of one who obviously has his own will to believe, we follow it with the judgment of a biologist whose heart is in the opposite, evolutionary camp. "I firmly believe," writes Jean Rostand,

> that mammals have come from lizards, and lizards from fish, but . . . when I think such a thing, I try not to avoid seeing its indigestible enormity and I prefer to leave vague the origin of these

15. *Mind*, LXX, 277 (Jan. 1961), 99.

scandalous metamorphoses rather than add to their improbability that of a ludicrous interpretation.[16]

Though this judgment has the merit of being that of a professional, it too is vulnerable. Rostand is but one biologist among many; for what proportion of his guild does he speak? So we round off the matter with a prediction: In the next hundred years, possibly less,[17] the fate of the evolutionary hypothesis will constitute the most interesting exemplification of the thesis Thomas Kuhn sets forth in *The Structure of Scientific Revolutions*; the thesis that scientists' need to make sense of their data causes them to continue to pour it into the prevailing mold (explanatory paradigm) until an alternative mold is fashioned that can accommodate the data more comfortably. When the change does occur, it does so quite suddenly. The picture "does a flip," as when one visual gestalt replaces another.

With this prediction we leave the empirical side of the evolutionary question; the data that would have to be sifted is, as we say, too vast to go into here. On the formal side, however, another point can be registered. If it is not entirely (or even primarily) evidence that gives the evolutionary hypothesis its seeming strength, from whence does that semblance derive? We have already mentioned man's need for hope as one explanation. To this we must now add a second that relates to the scientific enterprise itself.

A Cambridge University professor points to it. In reviewing a book on natural selection around midcentury, Sir James Gray wrote: "No amount of argument or clever epigram can disguise

16. *Le Figaro Littéraire*, April 20, 1957. Quoted in Burckhardt, "Cosmology and Modern Science," p. 143.

17. In the several weeks that have elapsed since those words were written, there have been signs that the time span in question may be closer to a decade than a century. Most interesting has been the appearance of Tom Bethell's "Darwin's Mistake" in the February 1976 issue of *Harper's Magazine* (pp. 72, 75). His conclusion is as follows: "Darwin's theory, I believe, is on the verge of collapse. . . . He is in the process of being discarded, but perhaps in deference to the venerable old gentleman, resting comfortably in Westminster Abbey next to Sir Isaac Newton, it is being done as discreetly and gently as possible, with a minimum of publicity."

the inherent improbability of [the orthodox evolutionary theory], but most biologists think that it is better to think in terms of improbable events than not to think at all."[18] It being axiomatic in science that one of the best ways "not to think" is by begging the question—that is, by assuming within an explanation that which it purports to explain—the first test a scientific explanation of the origin of life forms must pass is that the operative forces it invokes must not themselves possess life properties. This initial test Darwinism passes brilliantly: neither "chance" nor "the survival of those best suited to survive" presuppose the slightest intentionality or tropism. And because natural selection is the only hypothesis about life's origin that does pass this qualifying examination, it can fail right and left on subsequent tests (How much positive evidence supports it? Can it account for countervailing instances?) without losing its place as king of the mountain. For biologists are not different from other people; as Sir James says, they would rather shoulder improbabilities than not think (in their terms, by their criteria) at all.

In a brilliant paper prepared for the founding meeting of the Society for the Philosophy of Psychology (Massachusetts Institute of Technology, October 26, 1974), D. C. Dennett lays all this out clearly. Titled "Why the Law of Effect Will Not Go Away," the paper focuses on cognitive psychology but is relevant here by virtue of the explicit way it relates the Law of Effect to Darwinism. In the general terms in which Thorndike introduced that law, it holds that actions followed by reward are repeated. It is not a particularly good law; as Dennett says, its history has been "the history of ever more sophisticated failures to get [it] to *do enough work*."[19] Despite this, its tenacity exceeds that of old generals; it refuses not only to retire but to fade away. Periodically it is given a new title— the Law of Primary Reinforcement (Hull), the Principle of

18. *Nature*, CLXXIII, 4397 (Feb. 6, 1954), 227.
19. *Journal of the Theory of Social Behaviour*, V, 2 (1976), 172. Subsequent page references in the text are to this article.

Operant Conditioning (Skinner)—but rather than improving its performance these honorifics merely kick it upstairs, so to speak. Whence, then, its extraordinary lien on life? "It is not just mulishness or proproprietary pride," says Dennett, "that has kept behaviorists from . . . look[ing] for another fundamental principle of more power . . . but rather something like the conviction that the Law of Effect is not just *a* good idea, but the only possible good idea for this job" of explaining intelligence (p. 172). "There is something right in this conviction," Dennett continues, that something being that it is the only idea that has been proposed that does not beg the question. But there is also something wrong with the idea. And

> what is wrong in it has had an ironic result: allegiance to the Law of Effect in its behavioristic or peripheralistic versions has forced psychologists to beg small questions left and right in order to keep from begging the big question. One "saves" the Law of Effect from persistent counterinstances by the *ad hoc* postulation of reinforcers and stimulus histories for which one has not the slightest grounds except the demands of the theory. [p. 173]

The reason for this cross-reference to psychology is, to repeat, that "the Law of Effect is closely analogous to the principle of natural selection," having been, indeed, consciously modeled after it. From a "population" of stimulus-response pairs, born of random responses to a given stimulus, the nervous system reinforces pairs that are adaptive. This "selects" them by increasing the probability that they will recur "while their maladaptive or merely neutral brethren suffer 'extinction,' not by being *killed* (all particular stimulus-response pairs come to swift ends), but by *failing to reproduce*. The analogy [to Darwinism] is very strong, very satisfying, and very familiar." It is equally strong in the so-called dry, as opposed to biological or wet, approach to the study of learning and intelligence, the science of Artificial Intelligence which works with "thinking machines." Problem-solving computer programs are designed to generate and test. At a given point or points, the program sets up generating and testing units. The generating unit invents candidates for the problem's solution and transmits them to the testing unit, which accepts or rejects them on the basis of stored criteria. This again is like natural selection, as Herbert Simon points out.[20] Artificial Intelligence and cognitive psychology work from opposite ends of the scale. Artificial Intelligence begins with mechanisms that obviously lack intelligence—magnetic tapes whose segments do or do not conduct electrical currents—and tries to construct intelligence from these, whereas cognitive psychology begins with creatures that obviously have intelligence and tries to work back to neuron firings, nerve reflexes, and selector mechanisms that are as mechanical as computer operations. But forward or backward, the object is the same: to derive intelligence from things that do not possess it in the least. For

> psychology must not of course be question-begging. It must not explain intelligence in terms of intelligence, for instance by assigning responsibility for the existence of intelligence in creatures to the munificence of an intelligent Creator, or by putting clever homunculi at the control panels of the nervous system. If that were the best psychology could do, then psychology could not do the job assigned it. [p. 171]

The same holds for biology. The attraction of natural selection is that it seeks to

> provide clearly non-question-begging accounts. Darwin explains a world of final causes and teleological laws with a principle that is utterly independent of "meaning" or "purpose." It assumes a world that is *absurd* in the existentialist's sense of the term: not ludicrous but pointless, and this assumption is a necessary condition of any non-question-begging account of *purpose*. [pp. 171–72]

In sentences that are remarkable for the light they throw on the life sciences as enterprises—how they proceed, and how their procedures affect their findings by stipulating the kind of

20. *The Sciences of the Artificial* (Cambridge: M.I.T. Press, 1969), pp. 95–98.

findings that will be accepted—Dennett sums up the matter as follows:

> Whether we can imagine a *non*-mechanistic but also non-question-begging principle for explaining design in the biological world is doubtful; it is tempting to see the commitment to non-question-begging accounts here as tantamount to a commitment to mechanistic materialism, but the priority of these commitments is clear. It is not that one's prior prejudice in favor of materialism gives one reason to accept Darwin's principle because it is materialistic, but rather that one's prior acknowledgment of the constraint against begging the question gives one *reason to adopt materialism* once one sees that Darwin's non-question-begging account of design or purpose in nature is materialistic. One argues: Darwin's materialistic theory may not be the only non-question-begging theory of these matters, but it is one such theory, and the only one we have found, which is quite a good reason for espousing materialism. [p. 172]

To what degree this entire approach is likely to succeed—life out of nonlife, intelligence out of its absence, explanation out of that which in no way contains that which is to be explained —cannot, of course, be simply adjudicated. The question is fundamental; in a way the whole swing from tradition to modernity turns on it, and the point of this book is to help tip the lever back to its earlier, more natural, we contend, position. Charges of begging the question can settle nothing here, for the *petitio* is not a fallacy in the *form* of an argument; to invoke it, therefore, when the question concerns the truth-status of an argument's material premises or unvoiced assumptions is to commit the very fallacy that is being charged. Apart from material considerations, it is doubtful that the fallacy can even be clearly stated. An inquiry to a colleague in logic requesting a definition of the fallacy of begging the question brings word that the subject is in dispute and references to three current journal articles. Hoping to avoid this detour which looks as though it could lead into a bog, we ask what he would say if a student were to ask him straightforwardly what that fallacy *is*.

He answers: "I would tell him no clear formulation of it exists."

We were trying to account for the inflated status of the evolutionary hypothesis and have found thus far, beyond the way it buttresses hope, a methodological reason: the fact that it is the only candidate that meets the formal requirements for being scientific lets it get by with less supporting data than would otherwise be required. A corresponding ontological reason is that in the world with which science works, there is nowhere else to *look* for life's origin. Paraphrasing Sir James of a few pages back, we can say that if scientists prefer to think improbably than not to think at all, they would likewise rather pull rabbits out of hats than out of thin air, literally *ex nihilo*. From this second, ontological angle, we can join Burckhardt in ascribing part of evolutionism's force to "an incapacity—pecular to modern science—to conceive 'dimensions' of reality other than those of purely physical sequences; to understand the 'vertical' genesis of species."[21]

What is this vertical genesis of species? If we were to answer "God" this would not be incorrect, but the doctrine of "special creation" has become so weighted down with anthropomorphic imagery that we do better here to use its less personalized variant. The nonanthropomorphic counterpart of special creation is emanation. In the celestial realm the species are never absent; their essential forms or archetypes reside there from an endless beginning. As earth ripens to receive them, each in its turn drops[22] to the terrestrial plane and, donning the world's fabric, gives rise to a new life form. The origin of species is metaphysical.

First a viable habitat must be devised, hence the inorganic universe is matured to the point where life can be sustained. And when living beings do arrive, they do so in a vaguely as-

---

21. "Cosmology and Modern Science," p. 147.

22. After Chapter 2 on "The Symbolism of Space," we use words like this comfortably, trusting that the reader will not impute false literalisms to them.

cending order that passes from relatively undifferentiated organisms—though not simple ones; the electron microscope shows unicellular organisms to be astonishingly complicated—to ones that are more complex. But there is no need to force the fossil record to show a univocal and continuous line. If the movement proceeds in jumps with whole categories of plants and animals bursting out at once without discernible predecessors, this presents no problem. There is no need to multiply hypotheses by positing a thread that unites the various classes of life, such as insect, fish, reptile, bird, and mammal. We need not strain to see in the fins by which certain fishes flap their ways on shore rudiments of the articulation that arms and paws require but which fins show no beginnings of. Nor exaggerate the resemblance of birds to reptiles in an effort to prove that one derived from the other, an exercise that must proceed in the face of glaring differences in skeletal structure and the fact that the hearing apparatuses in the two orders are modeled on altogether different plans. If the tortoise turns up all at once in fossil remains or the spider appears simultaneously with its prey and with its faculty of weaving fully developed, such facts can be welcomed with smiles instead of puzzled brows.

As for the variant forms which Darwinists must use to construct their largely hypothetical bridges between species, from the metaphysical perspective these appear as variations which the species in question allow. It is as if nature, always more prolific and life-loving than we had supposed, first staked out distinct species and then decided to ring changes on these by having each reflect the forms of the others insofar as it could do so without transgressing its own essential limits. Seen in this light, variations are not generative links between species—it has yet to be shown what the dolphin, say, is a link to or from. They are, rather, mimics; they show species imitating the ways and forms of species that in essence are foreign to them. Not solely for utilitarian reasons of adaptation and survival, we may add; in part—larger part—for *lila*, the divine play:

sheer protean exuberance. *Esse qua esse* so *bonum est* (being as being is so good) that God cannot resist any of its possibilities. Wishing with part of herself to be a mother, a child dons apron and suckles her doll. Dolphins and whales are the archetypal mammal wondering what it would be like to be a fish; armadillos the result of its thinking, "Wouldn't it be interesting to dress up in scales and play reptile?"[23] Pressing the image a bit, we might say that hummingbirds in their mode of feeding and flight and their iridescent coloring are birds fancying themselves as butterflies. It is like Indra's Net, each jewel reflecting the others and being reflected in them.

Admitting that, to revert to an earlier image, we are performing here like the generating unit of a computer and not its testing unit, we push on to venture that the skeletons that evolutionists take to be protohuman may in fact be posthuman. They may be the deposits of degenerate epigones, tail ends of earlier human cycles *(yugas)* that were drawing to their close. After all, myths recount devolution more than evolution, and we know for a fact that later human forms are not necessarily more advanced: Steinheim man preceded Neanderthal but was more "evolved." If it be asked, "Where, then, are the remains of these 'giants who walked the earth in those days'?" it might be answered that in his beginnings, when he stood close to provenient spirit, man was ethereal to the point of leaving less in the way of ossified remains.

If this seems altogether too fantastic, we can at least take satisfaction in the fact that at last we have delivered on the promise with which we introduced this subject of human origins, the promise that we would say something faintly scandalous. If in doing so we have gone too far—so far perhaps as to cause the reader to close the book—it is not without design that we have reserved these speculations for the book's

23. We are speaking in the mode of Platonic myth, one consequence of which is that the reader will not be able to determine how literally we intend such statements because we are not sure ourselves. All we feel confident of is that they contain more truth than the alternatives they intend to counter.

closing chapter. In defense we say but this. Though we have not been unserious in anything we have postulated, the point we are most convinced of is the following: Whatever the utility of contemporary biological models for discovering useful specifics like antibiotics, for the *understanding* of life these models are largely useless. Moreover, they mislead.[24] The first shall be last and the last first, we are told. We have seen how in the microcosm/macrocosm mirror inversion, this decrees that man, who is first in the order of worth on the terrestrial plane, will be last in the order of his appearance. Now the converse: the last shall be first. Among the sciences, physics is ontologically the lowliest: it treats of matter in its most elementary arrangements. Concomitantly it is the first of the empirical sciences to "see through" its subject to a glimmering beyond. It *knows* the derivative character of space and time; the unimageable, transcendent character of the real. Even assuming that in specifics and details what we have ourselves postulated in these pages may be quite mistaken, we feel certain of this: if modern science continues, the current working premises in biology, Darwinism included, will in time (possibly quite a short time) show themselves to have been as inadequate as were Newton's. The life sciences will crash through them as through a sound barrier. On that glad day biologists will begin to talk like physicists. Like Richard Feynman, say: "We have to find a new view of the world." Or Freeman Dyson: "For any speculation which does not at first look crazy, there is no hope."

At last we have completed our excursus on evolution. As it has monopolized the better part of this chapter on hope, we trust that its object has not been lost from view. With the buckling of science and technology as props for the idea of progress, evolution has become its principal support. (This accounts for the emotional investment in Teilhard de Chardin.

---

24. "Though modern scientific knowledge reveals much that was previously unknown, . . . it hides or supplants much more." Lord Northbourne, *Looking Back on Progress* (London: Perennial Books, 1970), p. 116. The present chapter is deeply indebted to this lucid little book.

We know of no other twentieth-century thinker who has an entire journal devoted to the propagation of his theses.) Part of us feels bad about disturbing this prop, for in an age that has sealed over other outlets for hope, to undermine *evolution*, the last remaining prop for *progress*, which in the modern world has become the last remaining refuge for *hope*, is to undermine hope itself, and hope is indispensable to human well-being; this was this chapter's opening premise. But truth or consequences—when one must choose between them, jnana yogins at least, those whose approach to God (Reality) is by way of knowledge (gnosis), will understand that choice must favor the former. If within this vast universe a thread of life were to angle always upward, leaving a trail that looked from a distance like the jet stream of an ascending plane, such a never-circling life force would be a freak. For everywhere else —name one exception—nature favors the curves that space itself conforms to; the yin-yang rhythms of turning gyres and waves that crest and fall. O my people! can you not see how it is hope, not fact, that powers this dream of onward and upward toward the dawning light? If human life is truly natural —and this, surely, the evolutionists would want us to believe— it is seasonal. Fall and winter are its lot as assuredly as summer and spring. Half the art of living is a talent for dying.

Its other half, of course, is its talent for living, and this requires above all else an inward eye. Body dies, but the soul and spirit that animate it live on in ways that can be inferred from the Levels of Selfhood as described in Chapter 4. At death man is ushered into the unimaginable expanse of a reality no longer fragmentary but total. Its all-revealing light shows up his earthly career for what it truly was, and the revelation comes at first as judgment. The pretenses, rationalizations, and delusions that structured and warped his days are now glaringly evident. And because the self is now identified with its Mind or vital center rather than its Body as these terms were employed in Chapter 4, Mind's larger norms, to which the embodied ego paid little more than lip service, now hold the balance. It is thus that in hell man condemns himself; in the Koran it is his own members that rise up to accuse him. Once the self is extracted from the realm of lies, the falsities by which it armored itself within that realm become like flames and the life it there led like a shirt of Nessus.[25] When the flames have consumed these falsities—or to use other language, when truth has set the distortions of terrestrial existence in perspective—the balance is restored and the distortions, too, are seen to have had their place. This is forgiveness. With it, the Mind recedes as the Body earlier did at death, and the self, which is to say attention and identification, passes to the Soul's immortal center, which is now freed for the beatific vision. Lost in continual adoration and wonder, it abides in the direct presence of the Living God who is Being Itself. Beyond this, where the film that separates knower from known is itself removed and the self sinks into the Spirit that *is* the Infinite. . . . Ah, but we can say no more. We have reached the Cloud of Unknowing, where the rest is Silence.

If this sounds "old-fashioned," we trust that those who make this charge are not blind to the fact that it is the tacit progress-premise underlying that word that has turned it into a pejorative. We need not romanticize the past. If the most primitive people now living on the earth are also its sweetest and gentlest,[26] there are other primitives who are sadists. And

25. "The experience of death resembles that of a man who has lived all his life in a dark room and suddenly finds himself transported to a mountain top; there his gaze would embrace all the wide landscape; the works of men would seem insignificant to him. It is thus that the soul torn from the earth and from the body perceives the inexhaustible diversity of things and the incommensurable abysses of the worlds which contain them; for the first time it sees itself in its universal context, in an inexorable concatenation and in a network of multitudinous and unsuspected relationships, and takes account of the fact that life had been but an 'instant', but a 'play'. Projected into the absolute 'nature of things' man is inescapably aware of what he is in reality; he knows himself ontologically and without deforming perspective in the light of the normative 'proportions' of the Universe." F. Schuon, *Understanding Islam* (Baltimore: Penguin Books, 1972), p. 85.

26. John Nance, *The Gentle Tasaday* (New York: Harcourt Brace Jovanovich, 1975).

as for history, it shows grotesque aberrations as well as mag-
nificent achievements; we do not have to be reminded of tyran-
nies of altar and throne, the rigidities of imperial legalisms,
or the closedness of respectable mores and the sectarian spirit.
It is only in cosmic outlook that we see the past as superior to
ourselves and qualified to be our teacher; there may be other
ways, but we have not tried to sift the record. That there have
been in this world, and are today in lingering pockets, metaphysical doctrines that are complete along with means for their
realization—this is a notion that for moderns is barely conceivable, but it has emerged as the thesis of this book. In this
day of neophilia and reflective embrace of the new, when
"What's new?" has become standard salutation and quipsters
tell us they want even their antiques to be of the latest variety;
in this time when clergy themselves have grown "trendy" in
worship of their God who is "not yet" (Moltmann); this age
of flourishing futurists when almost the only way to get attention is to claim to be privy to some new discovery, it gives us
the most exceptional pleasure, the most piquant delight, to
announce what in today's climate of opinion may be the most
novel, original, and unexpected prediction imaginable. The
wave of the future will be a return to the past. "There is only
the fight to recover what has been lost / And found and lost
again and again."[27] "I sing the songs of olden times with
adoration."[28]

27. T. S. Eliot, "Four Quartets: East Coker," *The Complete Poems and Plays, 1909–1950* (New York: Harcourt, Brace & World, 1952), p. 128.
28. Svetasvatara Upanishad, II.5.

The master said, Who expects to be able to go
out of a house except by the door? How is it then
that no one follows this Way of ours?

CONFUCIUS, *Analects*, VI.15

7. Epilogue

Truth, Elie Wiesel has reminded us, is betrayed by its
repetition. Insofar as things have been said, there is no need
to resay them. Is there anything respecting our thesis that has
not been said and needs to be said?

Perhaps some misunderstandings can be anticipated and
allayed.

Our equation of tradition with norm, of what is inherited
(*traditio*, to hand over) with what should be espoused, may
sound to some like a counsel to "turn back the clocks"—as if
history could ever be reversed or an old man grow young again.
If we have left the impression that the primordial philosophy
counsels reversion, we should speak more plainly. The needed
return—a kind of homecoming—is in outlook only; it is in
world view and sense of reality, and even here phrases such as
"going back" are imprecise. For the issue does not really concern time at all; it concerns truth, truth of the kind that is
time*less*. If we have appealed to past ages it is because we see
them as having been bathed in such truth to a degree that we
are not. In this respect we would indeed be pleased to see life
on earth recover a lost dimension, and are grateful for persons
who are working to reknit the rich coherence of a fully human
consciousness which the cramped and aggressive rationality of
modernity has bruised so badly. But our opportunity is not in
any literal sense to go back, a move that in a thousand ways is
impossible even if it were desirable. Bygone days really are

gone, and many specifics of "the good old days" would not be good in our context.

What we might do is get back on course. This distinction between reverting to the past and realigning ourselves with the truth suggests a companion distinction respecting the word "original." The preceding chapter closed by alluding to the cult of originality which has become a hallmark of our time. We may now extend this allusion by pointing out that the kind of originality that has become fashionable—namely, that which feeds on difference and tokens departure—is limited to a single facet of the word; one, moreover, that is relatively late and superficial. Foundationally the word pointed in the opposite direction, to that which derives directly from its source or origin and is close to it, like water that is pure and uncontaminated by side influences and admixtures.

> The spacious firmament on high,
> With all the blue ethereal sky,
> And spangled heavens, a shining frame,
> Their great Original proclaim.[1]

"Originality is thus related to inspiration, and above all to revelation, for the origins are transcendent, being beyond this world, in the domains of Spirit. Ultimately the origin is nothing less than the Absolute, the Infinite and Eternal,"[2] and originality a guarantor of both authenticity and effectuality. In this fundamental sense of the word, a sense that carries the prospect of a progressive awakening in the direction of man's root and source, our book is a call for originality at all costs.

Developments will occur, of course; on the terrestrial plane nothing escapes change, and this holds as much for religions as for individuals and civilizations. Nor are changes in all respects

1. Joseph Addison, "Ode," in *The Spectator*, No. 465, Aug. 23, 1712. John Ruskin distinguishes the two senses of original as follows: "That virtue or originality that men so strain after is not *newness* (as they vainly think), it is only genuineness; it all depends on this single glorious faculty of getting to the spring of things and working out from that."

2. Martin Lings, *What Is Sufism?* (Berkeley: University of California Press, 1975), p. 15.

deleterious. Respecting religions, change often involves a double movement whose aspects to some extent balance one another. On the one hand the collectivity degenerates in proportion to its distance from the Revelation that launched it, while on the other hand, with respect to doctrine, the tradition blooms, values that were implicit from the start being now articulated. Thus a progressive and compensating unfolding occurs within the very framework of a general decline.[3] Five hundred years after the initial Vedic revelation, Brahmanism was in danger of ossifying in formalism and privilege: at precisely that moment the Upanishads appeared. Implicit wisdom was made explicit and rishis developed the techniques of yoga. Five hundred years after the Buddha, his tradition stood in like danger; it was on the verge of shriveling to a monasticism without possibility of expanding radiation. It was then that the Mahayana burgeoned, overlaying the "holy selfishness" of the Pratyeka Buddhas with the ideal of the compassionate Bodhisattva, and again the day was saved. In Judaism the time of the Psalms and the Song of Solomon could not possibly have been that of the Pentateuch, any more than the Kabbalah could have unfolded before the Middle Ages. The Christianity of the desert fathers flowers in the Middle Ages more gently under the sign of the Virgin Mother and gives rise in turn to pure gnosis in the Rhineland mystics and aspects of Scholasticism. In Islam the successive disintegration of empires and the sundering rift between Sunnis and Shi'ites are redeemed by the progressive unfolding of Sufism and the growth of its invigorating orders. It would be wrong to conclude from these examples that religions never decline

---

3. A similar pattern can often be seen in the history of art. "Strange as it may seem, it has always happened in the history of art, that by the time perfection of technique has been attained, inspiration has declined. It was so in Greece, and in Europe after the Renaissance. It almost seems as if concentration upon technique hindered the free working of the imagination a little; if so, however much we desire both, do not let us make any mistake as to which is first." A. K. Coomaraswamy, "The Aims of Indian Art," *Studies in Comparative Religion*, Winter 1975, p. 7.

and die. History shows that they do and logic that they must; belonging as they do to the order of finitude, their days are numbered from the start. The point of the illustrations is to correct a misreading this book might otherwise provoke: the mistake of assuming that the traditions teach that earlier is in every way better and the present without redeeming prospects of any sort.

A second misunderstanding could arise from the book's pronounced inwardness. A book of many silences, its silence on society is apt in these extroverted days to be particularly noticed and could raise the specter of social irresponsibility. On the question of how society might be benefited, tradition harbors insights almost equal to the ontological insights our pages have explored, beginning with its recognition that the issue is so complex that, depending on the context in question, the answer can range from jihad (holy warfare)[4] to *wu wei* ("the way to do is to be"). Obviously we are not going to get into this subject in an epilogue;[5] we note only that to charge the primordial perspective with social indifference is calumny. The fact that Confucius trudged for a decade trying to persuade rulers to convert his doctrines into practice, to say nothing of Muhammad, who in a relatively short time drew out of nothingness one of the greatest empires of history and a religion that has imposed and maintained itself on a quarter of the inhabited globe for nearly a millennium and a half— these facts alone should suffice to show that the issue tradition poses is not that of contemplation versus action or even sociopolitical action. In this area the issue is simply that of balance and proportion, the balance that derives from a sense *of* proportion, infinite matters being accorded infinite regard and finite ones being regarded conditionally. Christ tells us to "seek

4. Though even here Muhammad's characterization of overt physical combat as "the lesser jihad" must be remembered. "The greater jihad" is that directed against the foe within.

5. Gai Eaton's manuscript, "Choice and Responsibility," on which we have drawn a number of times in passing, will, if published, be a useful introduction to the topic.

. . . first the Kingdom," and even a tradition as occupied with society as is Confucianism observes that

> If there be righteousness in the heart, there will be beauty in the character.
>
> If there be beauty in the character, there will be harmony in the home.
>
> If there be harmony in the home, there will be order in the nation.
>
> If there be order in the nation, there will be peace in the world (*The Great Learning*).

It happened to have been Muhammad's destiny to penetrate versatilely an exceptionally wide range of earthy experience: not only was he shepherd, merchant, hermit, exile, soldier, lawgiver, and prophet-priest-king; he was also orphan (but with a remarkably loving grandfather and uncle), for many years the husband of one wife much older than himself, a many times bereaved father, a widower, and finally the husband of many wives, some much younger than himself.[6] What sanctified this earthly plenitude was the degree to which it was dominated by acute and unswerving sensitivity to the magnetism of the Hereafter. "Do for this world," he said, "as if thou wert to live a thousand years and for the next as if thou wert to die tomorrow." On the one hand this Hadith "enjoins the perfection—the patient thoroughness we might say—incumbent upon man as representative of God on earth: and on the other hand it demands that he shall be ready to leave this world at a moment's notice."[7] Inasmuch as this terrestrial plane is our current lot, it is not only natural but appropriate for us to feel concern for our daily problems and those of our neighbors. We build our sand castles because we need them, and in their small way they are beautiful, reflecting in their fragile moats and turrets the patterns of another place, a more enduring realm. But every man and woman is infinitely

6. Martin Lings, *What Is Sufism?* p. 34.
7. *Ibid.*

more than the child that plays thus in salt and sand, even as a seed contains in virtuality a great tree: "O high-born race of foreigners on earth . . . you do not belong here, you belong somewhere else."[8] Moreover, our entire visible cosmos rests on an invisible volcano. We imagine that our earth, its mountain ranges and unplumbed seas, can be destroyed only by forces of its own kind, by masses and energies that are in some way physical, but in this we are mistaken. The world, in appearance so resilient, so substantial, can withdraw "from within." Matter can flow back to the immaterial source from which it came, causing the entire space-time field to collapse like a balloon that is emptied of air. Our marvel consists in the fact that, possessed as we are of souls and Spirit, we can escape this collapse by retreating, or rather advancing, into the mathematical point, our unchanging Center which is non-spatial. All discussion of social problems and the dangers that press upon us should proceed in the context of this realization. They must be given their fair measure of concern but not more.

We said that the visible cosmos rests on an invisible volcano, but we must now add that at a deeper ontological level it floats on an ocean of bliss. The addition is needed to offset a third possible misunderstanding of the primordial outlook, the last that we shall mention: namely, that the view is pessimistic. At first glance it is difficult to take this supposition seriously: does a reader suppose that we would have taken the pains to write this book for the object of piping man into a gloomier mood than the one he now enjoys? we impulsively wonder.[9] On second thought, however, one sees how charges of pessimism

---

8. Augustine, *Enarrationes in Psalmos*, 136.13.
9. "Freud's very pessimism and cynicism is still the most contemporary thing about his thought," Ernest Becker wrote in *The Denial of Death* (New York: Free Press, 1973), p. 94. As a barometric reading, the sentence would be worth quoting had it ended there, but the way it continues makes it interesting in another respect: ". . . it is a pessimism grounded in reality, in scientific truth," Becker concludes. We have ourselves said many things about science in this book; none, we trust, as irresponsible as this.

and failure of nerve arise. If optimism requires (on its negative side) refusal to accept imperfection as an inherent feature of the terrestrial world, or (stated positively) faith in historical progress, optimism is indeed unavailable to the traditions. But only a logic that is blind to alternatives could conclude from this that the traditions are pessimistic in their own right. Characterizing the South Asian formulation of the primordial outlook, Heinrich Zimmer writes:

> Philosophical theory, religious belief, and intuitive experience support each other . . . in the basic insight that, fundamentally, all is well. A supreme optimism prevails everywhere, in spite of the unromantic recognition that the universe of man's affairs is in the most imperfect state imaginable, one amounting practically to chaos.[10]

Toward the middle of this book we said that at heart what sets us against modernity is its determination, scientistically derived, to reverse tradition's premise and explain the more in terms of the less. Even there we noted the inevitable though subtle consequence of this reversal: the more becomes lessened by the etiology. Now, at the book's close, we focus on this consequence itself and say that what sets us against modernity is its demeaning of the human potential. The primordial tradition holds that man—not man in some hypothetically envisioned future, but man as he is constituted today and has always been constituted—is heir to *Sat*, *Chit*, and *Ananda*: Infinite Being, Infinite Awareness, Infinite Bliss. It is impossible in principle for any alternative, ancient or modern, to match that claim, for if it did, in essence it would *be* the primordial philosophy, however different its details. In Dante's *Inferno* souls have what they choose. The fate of those he classifies as "virtuous pagans" derives from nothing more than their failure to imagine better.

The traditions are realistic. Buddha saw the waters of the seas as but a drop compared with the tears men have shed since

10. *The Philosophies of India* (New York: Pantheon Books, 1951), p. 549.

they reached the earth: "I teach ill," he said. But we know that his assertion did not end there; "I teach ill and the ending of ill," it continued. Our world is by definition a grimy, flawed, and broken place; it is subject to decay and riddled with death. If it were otherwise, it would be indistinguishable from the timeless perfection of Paradise and would forfeit its separate existence. Yet with all its deformities it can be rendered transparent, and perfection can be discerned behind its shapes and patterns; it can also be loved in a way that turns its flaws themselves into objects of redeeming compassion. This is the spiritual counterpart of the fact that with all its smog and pollution, our planet rides in an ocean of sunlight through the innermost recesses of the solar system. Being is woven of beatitude; there is a Buddha in every grain of sand.

"The world," said St. Augustine, "is a smiling place." As for the Celestial City to which it is antechamber, "Brethren, when I speak of that City . . . I just cannot bring myself to stop. . . ."[11] The only way *to* stop is to modulate discernment to heights where words, having reached their timberline, can go no further.

> Guide us to that topmost height of mystic lore which exceedeth light and more than exceedeth knowledge, where the simple, absolute, and unchangeable mysteries of heavenly Truth lie hidden in the dazzling obscurity of the secret Silence, outshining all brilliance with the intensity of their darkness, and surcharging our blinded intellects with the utterly impalpable and invisible fairness of glories which exceed all beauty! Such be my prayer.[12]

11. *Sermon,* 158.7; *Enarrationes in Psalmos,* 136.13.
12. Dionysius the Areopagite, *The Divine Names and The Mystical Theology* (London: S.P.C.K., 1971), p. 191.

ADDENDUM

Daniel Ellsberg, reading this book in page proofs, has called my attention to something worth stopping the presses for. On pages 41 and 129, in pointing out tradition's inversion of the modern propensity to derive the more from the less, the better from sources that are inferior, I cited the Marxist contention that order derives from chaos. This is, of course, the way Marxism is read; it looks toward a classless society while asserting as the opening claim of *The Communist Manifesto* that "The history of all hitherto existing society is the history of class struggles." But that was written in 1847. Forty-one years later the findings of the anthropologists had advanced to the point where they could not be ignored, and Engels was forced to append a footnote. Thus, to the sentence just quoted the 1888 edition adds, "That is, all *written* history."

In view of the ratio of unwritten to written history, it is just possible that no other footnote, ever penned, retracts so much.

Appendix:
The Psychedelic Evidence

Know ten things, the Chinese say; tell nine—there is reason to question whether it is wise even to mention the psychedelics in connection with God and the Infinite. For though a connection exists, it is—as in the comparable case of the role of sex in Tantra—next to impossible to speak of it without being misunderstood. It is for this reason, we suspect, that the Eleusinian mysteries were among the best-kept in history, and Brahmins came eventually to conceal, then deliberately forget, the identity of soma.[1]

If the only thing to say about the psychedelics was that they seem on occasion to offer direct disclosures of the psychic and celestial planes as well as (in rare instances) the Infinite itself, we would hold our peace. For though such experiences may be veridical in ways, the goal, it cannot be stressed too often, is not religious experiences; it is the religious life. And with respect to the latter, psychedelic "theophanies" can abort a quest as readily as, perhaps more readily than, they can further it.

It is not, therefore, the isolated mystical experiences which the psychedelics can occasion that lead us to add this appendix on the subject, but rather evidence of a different order. Long-term, professionally garnered and carefully weighed, this latter evidence deserves to be called, if anything in this area merits the term, scientific. We enter it because of the ways in which, and extent to which, this evidence seems to corroborate the primordial anthropology that Chap-

1. See the author's "Wasson's *SOMA*: A Review Article," *Journal of the American Academy of Religion*, XL, 4 (Dec. 1972).

ter 4 sketched in paradigm. In contradistinction to writings on the psychedelics which are occupied with experiences the mind can *have*, the concern here is with evidence they afford as to what the mind *is*.[2]

The evidence in question is not widely known, for to date it has been reported only in a few relatively obscure journals and a book but recently off the press. At the same time, judged both by quantity of data encompassed and by the explanatory power of the hypotheses that make sense of this data, it is the most formidable evidence the psychedelics have thus far produced. The evidence to which we refer is that which has emerged through the work of Stanislav Grof.[3]

Grof's work began in Czechoslovakia, where for four years he worked in an interdisciplinary complex of research institutes in Prague and for another seven in the Psychiatric Research Institute that developed out of this complex; on coming to the United States in 1967 he continued his investigations at the Research Unit of Spring Grove State Hospital in Baltimore, Maryland. Two covering facts about his work are worth noting before we turn to its content. First, in the use of psychedelics for therapeutic and personality assessment, his experience is by far the vastest that any single individual has amassed, covering as it does over 2,500 sessions in which he spent a minimum of five hours with the subject. In addition his studies cover another 800 cases his colleagues at Baltimore and Prague conducted. Second, in spanning the Atlantic his work spans the two

2. "LSD, the most powerful psycho-active drug ever known to man, is essentially an unspecific amplifier of mental processes. What we see in LSD sessions is only an exteriorization and magnification of dynamics that underlie human nature and human civilization. Properly used, the drug is a tool for a deeper understanding of the human mind and human nature." Abridged from the writings of Stanislav Grof, cited in footnote 3.

3. His book, the first in a projected five-volume series, is *Realms of the Human Unconscious: Observations from LSD Research* (New York: Viking Press, 1975). His journal articles are: "Beyond Psychoanalysis: I. Implications of LSD Research for Understanding Dimensions of Human Personality," *Darshana International* (India, 1970); "LSD Psychotherapy and Human Culture," *Journal of the Study of Consciousness*, Part I, 1970, Part II, 1971; "The Use of LSD in Psychotherapy," *Journal of Psychedelic Drugs*," 1970; "Varieties of Transpersonal Experiences: Observations from LSD Psychotherapy," *Journal of Transpersonal Psychology*, 1972; "LSD and the Cosmic Game: Outline of Psychedelic Cosmology and Ontology," *Journal of the Study of Consciousness*, 1972; and one more which, because it is his latest paper, will be quoted most often in this chapter. It is cited in footnote 4.

dominant approaches to psychedelic therapy that have been developed: psycholytic therapy (used at Prague and favored in Europe generally), which involves numerous administrations of low to medium doses of LSD or variant over a long therapeutic program, and psychedelic therapy (confined to America), which involves one or a few high doses in a short period of treatment.

The first thing Grof and his associates discovered was that there is no specific pharmacological effect which LSD invariably produces: "I have not been able to find a single phenomenon that could be considered an invariant product of the chemical action of the drug in any of the areas studied—perceptual, emotional, ideational, and physical."[4] Not even mydriasis (prolonged dilatation of the pupils), one of the most common symptoms, occurs invariably. Psychological effects vary even more than do physiological, but the range of the latter—mydriasis, nausea, and vomiting, enhanced intestinal movements, diarrhea, constipation, frequent urination, acceleration as well as retardation of pulse, cardiac distress and pain, palpitations, suffocation and dyspnea, excessive sweating and hypersalivation, dry mouth, reddening of the skin, hot flushes and chills, instability and vertigo, inner trembling, fine muscle tremors—exceeds that of any other drug that affects the autonomic nervous system. These somatic symptoms are practically independent of dosage and occur in all possible combinations. Variability between subjects is equaled by variation in the symptoms a single subject will experience under different circumstances; particularly important from the clinical point of view are the differences that appear at different stages in the therapeutic process. All this led Grof to conclude that LSD is not a specific causal agent, but rather a catalyzer. It is, as footnote 2 indicates, an unspecific amplifier of neural and mental processes. By exteriorizing for the therapist and raising to consciousness for the patient himself material otherwise buried, and by enlarging this material to the point of caricature so that it appears as if under a magnifying glass, the psychedelics are, Grof became convinced, an

4. "Theoretical and Empirical Basis of Transpersonal Psychology and Psychotherapy: Observations from LSD Research," *Journal of Transpersonal Psychology*, 1973. Unless otherwise indicated, subsequent references in this appendix will be to this, Grof's latest paper. Also, though his work covers a wide spectrum of psychedelic substances, most of it was with LSD, so we shall limit our references to it.

unrivaled instrument: first, for identifying causes in psychopathology (the problem that is causing the difficulty); second, for personality diagnosis (determining the character type of the subject in question); and third, for understanding the human mind generally. "It does not seem inappropriate to compare their potential significance for psychiatry and psychology to that of the microscope for medicine or of the telescope in astronomy. . . . Freud called dreams the 'royal way to the unconscious.' The statement is valid to a greater extent for LSD experiences."[5]

Of the drug's three potentials, it is the third—its resources for enlarging our understanding of the human mind and self—that concerns us in this book. The nature of man has been so central to our study that even flickers of light from Grof's work would make it interesting. That the light proves to be remarkably clear and steady makes it important.

We come at once to the point. The view of man that was outlined in Chapter 4 presented him as a multilayered creature, and Grof's work points to the same conclusion. As long as the matter is put thus generally it signals nothing novel, for existing depth psychology —psychiatry, psychoanalysis—says the same; the adjective "depth" implies as much, and metaphors of archaeology and excavation dot the writings of Freud, Jung, and their colleagues. The novelty of Grof's work lies in the precision with which the levels of the mind it brings to view correspond with the levels of selfhood the primordial tradition describes.

In chemo-excavation the levels come to view sequentially. In this respect, too, images of archaeology apply: surface levels must be uncovered to get at ones that lie deeper. In psychedelic (high-dose) therapy the deeper levels appear later in the course of a single session; in psycholytic (low-dose) therapy they surface later in the sequence of therapeutic sessions. The sequences are parallel, but since the levels first came to Grof's attention during his psycholytic work in Prague, and since that earlier work was the more extensive, covering eleven of the seventeen years he has been working with the

5. "Theory and Practice of LSD Psychotherapy" (U68). Instead of being published as a single volume as Grof originally intended, this long, initial report of his study is being reworked for projected issue in five volumes, the first of which, as indicated in footnote 3, appeared in 1975. Page references to the comprehensive original report will hereafter be prefixed with a U, indicating unpublished. Page numbers not thus prefixed refer to the paper named in footnote 4.

drugs, we shall confine ourselves to it in reporting his experimental design.

The basic study at Prague covered fifty-two psychiatric patients. All major clinical categories were represented, from depressive disorders through psychoneuroses, psychosomatic diseases, and character disorders to borderline and clear-cut psychoses in the schizophrenic group. Patients with above-average intelligence were favored to obtain high-quality introspective reports; otherwise cases with dim prognosis in each category were chosen. Grof himself worked with twenty-two of the subjects, his two colleagues with the remainder. The number of psycholytic sessions ranged from fifteen to one hundred per patient with a total of over 2,500 sessions being conducted. Each patient's treatment began with several weeks of drug-free psychotherapy. Thereafter the therapy was punctuated with doses of 100 to 250 micrograms of LSD administered at seven- to fourteen-day intervals.

The basic finding was that "when material from consecutive LSD sessions of the same person was compared it became evident that there was a definite continuity between these sessions. Rather than being unrelated and random, the material seemed to represent a successive unfolding of deeper and deeper levels of the unconscious with a very definite trend" (U41).

The trend regularly led through three successive stages preceded by another which, being less important psychologically, Grof calls a preliminary phase. In this opening phase the chemical works primarily on the subject's body. In this respect it resembles what earlier researchers had called the vegetative phase, but the two are not identical. Proponents of a vegetative phase assumed that LSD directly caused the manifold somatic responses patients typically experience in the early stages of psychedelic sessions. We have seen that Grof's more extensive evidence countered this view. Vegetative symptoms are real enough, but they vary so much between subjects and for a single subject under varying circumstances that it seems probable that they are occasioned more by anxieties and resistances than by the chemical's direct action. There is also the fact that they are far from confined to early phases of the LSD sequence. These considerations led Grof to doubt that there is a vegetative phase per se. The most he is prepared to admit is that the drug has a tendency at the start to affect one specific part of the body: its perceptual and particularly its optical apparatus. Colors become exceptionally bright and beautiful, objects and persons are geome-trized, things vibrate and undulate, one hears music as if one were somehow inside it, and so on. This is as close as the drug comes to producing a direct somatic effect, but it is sufficient to warrant speak-ing of an introductory phase which Grof calls aesthetic.

With this preliminary phase behind him the subject begins his psycholytic journey proper. Its first stage is occupied with material that is psychodynamic in the classical sense: Grof calls it the psy-chodynamic or Freudian stage. Experiences here are of a distinctly personal character. They involve regression into childhood and the reliving of traumatic infantile experiences in which Oedipal and Electra conflicts and ones relating to various libidinal zones are conspicuous; first and last, pretty much the full Freudian topogra-phy is traversed. The amount of unfinished business this layer of the self contains varies enormously; as would be expected, in disturbed subjects there is more than in normals. But the layer itself is present in everyone and must be worked through before the next stratum can be reached. "Worked through" again means essentially what psychiatry stipulates: a reliving not only in memory but in emotion of the traumatic episodes that have unconsciously crippled the patient's responses. Freud and Breuer's hypothesis that insufficient emotional and motor abreaction during early traumatic episodes pro-duces a "jamming" of affect that provides energy thereafter for neurotic symptoms is corroborated, for when patients in the course of a number of sessions enter into a problem area to the point of reliving it completely and integrating it into consciousness, the symptoms related to that area "never reappear" and the patient is freed to work on other symptoms.

This much was in keeping with Grof's psychiatric orientation; it came as "laboratory proof of the basic premises of psychoanalysis" (p. 21). But there that model gave out. For the experiences that fol-lowed, "no adequate explanation can be found within the framework of classical Freudian psychoanalysis" (pp. 24–25).[6]

6. On the limited range of the Freudian model I insert a supporting remark by Gordon Allport, in his latter years the dean of American per-sonality theorists. In his closing years at Harvard he would invite me to his seminars to register such light as Asian psychology might throw on human nature. One year I organized my remarks around India's "four psychologies," geared respectively to *kama* (pleasure), *artha* (wealth or worldly success), *dharma* (duty), and *moksha* (liberation). Allport's response

Negatively the new stage was characterized by an absence of the individually and biographically determined material that had dominated the sessions theretofore. As a result, the experiential content of this second stage was more uniform for the population than was the content of the first. We have already cited Grof's contention that LSD is not so much an agent that produces specific effects as it is an amplifier of material that is already present, and in the first stage the enlarging process worked to magnify individual differences: "the sessions of patients belonging to various diagnoistic categories were characterized by an unusual inter- and also intra-individual variability" (U118). In the second stage the process was reversed. With the magnifying glass still in place, variations receded. "The content seemed to be strikingly similar in all of the subjects" (*ibid.*).

This is already important, for the emergent similarity suggests that the subjects were entering a region of the mind which they shared in common, a region that underlay the differing scrawls their separate biographies had incised upon it. As to content, "the central focus and basic characteristics of the experience on this level are the problems related to physical pain and agony, dying and death, biological birth, aging, disease and decrepitude" (p. 25)—Buddha's First Noble Truth, Grof somewhere observes, and three of the Four Passing Sights that informed it. Inevitably, he continues,

> the shattering encounter with these critical aspects of human existence and the deep realization of the fraility and impermanence of man as a biological creature, is accompanied by an agonizing existential crisis. The individual comes to realize through these experiences that no matter what he does in his life, he cannot escape the inevitable: he will have to leave this world bereft of everything that he has accumulated, achieved and has been emotionally attached to. [*ibid.*]

Among the phenomena of this second stage the theme of death and rebirth recurred so frequently that it sent Grof to a book he had heard of in his psychiatric training but had not studied, it having been written by a psychoanalytic renegade, Otto Rank. It bore the

---

was: "In the West we have a detailed psychology of pleasure à la Freud's Pleasure Principle. McClelland's 'achievement motivation' has added to this a psychology of success. Respecting duty we have a nickel's worth of Freud's superego, and on the psychology of liberation—nothing."

title *The Trauma of Birth*, and to use Grof's own word, he was "flabbergasted" to find how closely the second-stage psycholytic experiences conformed to it. He and his colleagues fell to calling the second stage perinatal or Rankian.

During the weeks through which the stage extends, the patient's clinical condition worsens. The stage climaxes in a session in which the patient experiences the agony of dying and appears to himself actually to die.

> The subjects can spend hours in agonizing pain, with facial contortions, gasping for breath and discharging enormous amounts of muscular tension in various tremors, twitching, violent shaking and complex twisting movements. The color of the face can be dark purple or dead pale, and the pulse rate considerably accelerated. The body temperature usually oscillates in a wide range, sweating can be profuse, and nausea with projectile vomiting is a frequent occurrence. [*ibid.*]

This death experience tends to be followed immediately by rebirth, an explosive ecstasy in which joy, freedom, and the promise of life of a new order are the dominant motifs.

Outside the LSD sequence the new life showed itself in the patients' marked clinical improvement. Within the sequence it introduced a third experiential landscape. When Grof's eyes became acclimated to it, it appeared at first to be Jungian, Jung being the only major psychologist to have dealt seriously and relatively unreductionistically with the visions that appeared. Later it seemed clearer to refer to the stage as transpersonal.

Two features defined this third and final stage. First, its "most typical characteristics . . . were profound religious and mystical experiences" (U125).

> Everyone who experientially reached these levels developed convincing insights into the utmost relevance of spiritual and religious dimensions in the universal scheme of things. Even the most hardcore materialists, positivistically-oriented scientists, skeptics and cynics, uncompromising atheists and antireligious cruaders such as the Marxist philosophers, became suddenly interested in spiritual search after they confronted these levels in themselves. [p. 25]

Grof speaks of levels in the plural here, for the "agonizing existential crisis" of the second stage is already religious in its way: death and rebirth are ultimates or none exist. The distinguishing feature of the third stage is not, strictly speaking, that it is religious but that it is (as Grof's words indicate) mystically religious: religious in a mode in which (a) the whole predominates over the part, and (b) within the whole evil is rescinded. This connects with the stage's other feature, its transpersonal aspect, which was so pronounced as to present itself in the end as the logical candidate for the name by which the stage should be designated. A trend toward transpersonal experiences, that is, ones occupied with things other than oneself, had already shown itself in stage two. Suffering, for example, which in the first stage presented itself in the form of recollected autobiographical traumas, had in the second stage taken the form of identifying with the suffering of others, usually groups of others: famine victims, prisoners in Nazi concentration camps, or mankind as a whole with its suffering symbolized archetypally by Christ on his cross, Tantalus exposed to eternal tortures in Hades, Sisyphus rolling his boulder incessantly, Ixion fixed on his wheel, or Prometheus chained to his rock. Likewise with death; already by stage two "the subjects felt that they were operating in a framework which was 'beyond individual death' " (U125). The third stage continues this outbound, transpersonal momentum. Now the phenomena with which the subject identifies are not restricted to mankind or even to living forms. They are cosmic, having to do with the elements and forces from which life proceeds. And the subject is less conscious of himself as separate from what he perceives. To a large extent the subject-object dichotomy is itself transcended.

So much for description of the three stages. Now to interpretation and explanation.

Grof was and is a psychiatrist. Psychiatry is the study and practice of ontogenetic explanation: it accounts for present syndromes in terms of antecedent experiences in the life history of the individual. Freud had mined these experiences as they occur in infancy and childhood, but Grof's work had led to regions Freud's map did not fit. Clearly, as psychiatrist, Grof had nowhere to turn for explanations save further in the same direction—further back. His very methodology forced him to take seriously the possibility that experiences attending birth and even gestation could affect ensuing life trajectories.

Taking his cues from *The Trauma of Birth* while emending it in important respects, Grof worked out a typology in which second- and third-stage LSD experiences are correlated with four distinct stages in the birth process: (a) a comfortable, intrauterine stage before the onset of labor; (b) an oppressive stage at labor's start when the fetus suffers the womb's contractions and has "no exit" inasmuch as the cervix has not opened; (c) the traumatic ensuing stage of labor during which the fetus is violently ejected through the birth canal; and (d) the freedom and release of birth itself. B and c seemed to Grof to vector the second or Rankian stage in the LSD sequence. In the reliving of b, the oppressiveness of the womb is generalized and the entire world, existence itself, is experienced as oppressive. C, when relived—the agony of labor and forced expulsion through the birth canal—produces the experience of dying: traumatic ejection from the only life-giving context one has known. The rebirth experience in which the Rankian stage climaxes derives from reliving the experience of physical birth (d) and paves the way for the ensuing transpersonal stage. The sense of unshadowed bliss that dominates this final stage taps the earliest memories of all: before the womb grew crowded, when the fetus blended with its mother in mystic embrace (a).

Even in bare outline Grof's hypothesis is plausible, and when fleshed out with the case histories and experiential accounts that gave rise to it (material that is fascinating but which space precludes our entering here) it is doubly so. When subjects in their Rankian stage report first suffocation and then a violent, projective explosion in which not only blood but urine and feces are everywhere, one is persuaded that revived memories of the birth process play at least a part in triggering, shaping, and energizing later-stage LSD experiences. The question is: Are these the only causes at work? As we have noted, in the psychiatric model of man, once the Freudian domain has been exhausted there is nowhere to look for causes save where Rank did and Grof does: the ego, driven back to earlier and yet earlier libido positions, finally reenters the uterus. In the model of man that was sketched in Chapter 4, however, things are different. There the social and biological history of the organism is not the sole resource for explanation. "The soul that rises with us . . .

> Hath had elsewhere its setting,
>   And cometh from afar:
>   Not in entire forgetfulness . . .
> But trailing clouds of glory do we come. . . .

From whence? "From God," Wordsworth tells us, and we agree. When he adds in the line that follows: "Heaven lies about us in our infancy!" we again concur; as the celestial plane it envelops our souls not only in their infancy but always. More proximately, however, it is the intermediate or psychic plane from which we stem. Whereas in the psychiatric perspective body is basic and explanations for mental occurrences are sought in body's endowments or history, in the primordial psychology body represents a kind of shaking out of what has condensed on the plane of mental phenomena that exist prior to body and are more real than body. We are back at the point Chapter 4 made in the context of dreams: it is not so much that we dream as that we are dreamed, if we may use this way of saying that the forces that come to the fore in our dreams pull the strings that govern our puppet existences. They do not govern them entirely—man is man, not manikin—but to say that they govern them is closer to the truth than is the epiphenomenal view in which body pays the piper and calls the tunes that dreams play out.

Thus to Grof's finding that later stages in the LSD sequence conform to the stages of the birth process to a degree that warrants our saying that they are influenced by those stages, we add: influenced only, not caused. To a greater degree the experiences of these stages put the subject in direct touch with the psychic and archetypal forces of which his life is distillation and product. Birth and death are not physical only. Everyone knows this, but it is less recognized that physical birth and death are relatively minor manifestations of forces that are cosmic in blanketing the manifest world, the terrestrial and intermediate planes combined. Buddhism's *pratitya-samutpada* (Formulation of Dependent Origination) says profound things on this point, but all we shall say is that when a psychic quantum, germ of an ego, decides—out of ignorance, the Buddhists insert immediately—that it would be interesting to go it alone and have an independent career, in thereby distinguishing itself from the whole, and setting itself in ways against the whole, the ego shoulders certain consequences. Because it is finite, things will not always go its way: hence suffering in its manifold varieties. And the temporal side of the self's finitude ordains that it will die—piecemeal from the start as cells and minor dreams collapse, but eventually in its entirety. Energy is indestructible, however, so in some form there is rebirth. Confrontation of these principal truths in their transpersonal and trans-species scopes and intensity is the basic stuff of later-stage LSD experience. Biological memory enters, but conceivably with little more than a "me too": I too know the sequence from the time I was forged and delivered.

Spelled out in greater detail, the primordial explanation of the sequence would run as follows. Accepting LSD as a "tool for the study of the structure of human personality; of its various facets and levels," we see it uncovering the successively deeper layers of the self which Grof's study brings to light. Grof's psychiatric explanation for why it does so is that "defense systems are considerably loosened, resistances decrease, and memory recall is facilitated to a great degree. Deep unconscious material emerges into consciousness and is experienced in a complex symbolic way" (U277). Our explanation shifts the accent. Only in the first stage are the defense systems that are loosened ones that the individual ego builds to screen out painful memories. For the rest, what is loosened are structures that condition the human mode of existence and separate it from modes that are higher: its corporeality and compliance with the spatio-temporal structures of the terrestrial plane. The same holds for the memory recall that LSD facilitates. In the first stage it is indeed memory that is activated as the subject relives, directly or in symbolic guise, the experiences that had befallen it, but in later stages what the psychiatrist continues to see as memory—an even earlier, intrauterine memory—the ontologist (short of invoking reincarnation) sees as discovery: the discovery of layers of selfhood that are present from conception but are normally obscured from view. Likewise with the "peculiar double orientation and double role of the subject" that Grof describes. "On the one hand," he writes, the subject "experiences full and complex age regression into the traumatic situations of childhood; on the other hand, he can assume alternately or even simultaneously the position corresponding to his real age" (U279). This oscillation characterizes the entire sequence, but only in the first stage is its not-immediate referent the past. In the later sessions, that which is not immediate is removed not in time but in space—psychological space, of course. It lies below the surface of the exterior self that is normally in view.

The paradigm of the self that was sketched in Chapter 4 showed it to be composed of four parts: body, mind, soul, and Spirit. Working with spatial imagery, we can visualize LSD as a seeing-eye probe that penetrates progressively toward the core of the subject's being. In the early sessions of the LSD sequence it moves through the subject's *body* in two steps. The first of these triggers peripheral somatic responses, most regularly ones relating to perception, to produce the aesthetic phase. The second moves into memory regions of the brain where, Wilder Penfield has posited, a complete cinematographic record of everything the subject has experienced lies stored. That the events that were most important in the subject's formation are the ones that rush forward for attention stands to reason. We are into the first of the three main stages of the psycholytic sequence, the psychodynamic or Freudian stage.

Passage from the Freudian to the Rankian stage occurs when the chemicals enter the region of the mind that outdistances the brain and swims in the medium of the psychic or intermediate plane. The phenomenological consequences could almost have been predicted:

1. Biographical data—events that imprinted themselves on the subject's body, in this case the memory region of his brain—recede.

2. Their place is taken by the "existentials"—conditioning structures—of human existence in general. The grim affect of this stage could be due in part to memories of the ordeals of gestation and birth, but the torment, the sense of the wistfulness and pathos of a suffering humanity and indeed life in all its forms, derives mainly from the fact that the larger purview of the intermediate plane renders the limitations (*dukkha*) of the terrestrial plane more visible than when the subject is immersed in them.

3. In the death and rebirth experience that climaxes this phase, Rankian factors could again cooperate without precluding causes that are more basic. The self had entered the intermediate plane through the soul's assumption of—compression into—mind; as the Hindus say, the *jiva* assumed a subtle body. Now, in the reversal of this sequence, mind must be dissolved (die) for soul to be released (reborn).

The sense of release from the imprisoning structures of mind signals the fact that the probe has reached the level of *soul*. The phenomenological consequences are the ones Grof's subjects reported in the transpersonal stage, the main ones being the following:

1. Whereas in the Rankian stage "there . . . was . . . a very distinct polarity between very positive and very negative experience" (U125),

experience is now predominantly beatific, with "melted ecstasy" perhaps its most-reported theme. Subjects "speak about mystic union, the fusion of the subjective with the objective world, identification with the universe, cosmic consciousness, the intuitive insight into the essence of being, the Buddhist nirvanam, the Vedic samadhi, the harmony of worlds and spheres, the approximation to God, etc." (U29).

2. Experience is more abstract. At its peak it "is usually contentless and accompanied by visions of blinding light or beautiful colors (heavenly blue, gold, the rainbow spectrum, peacock feathers, etc.)" (ibid.) or is associated with space or sound. When its accouterments are more concrete they tend to be archetypal, with the archetypes seeming to be limitless in number. The celestial plane which the soul inhabits is, we recall, the plane of God and the archetypes. The distinction between the two, which if fleshed out would result in an ontology of five tiers instead of four (see footnote, page 51), is for purposes of simplification and symmetry being played down in the present book.

3. The God who is almost invariably encountered is single and so far removed from anthropomorphism as to elicit, often, the pronoun "it." This is in contrast to the gods of the Rankian stage which tend to be multiple, Olympian, and essentially enlarged titans.

Beyond the soul lies only *Spirit*, an essence so ineffable that when the seeing eye strikes it, virtually all that can be reported is that it is "beyond" and "more than" all that had been encountered theretofore.

The correlations between the primordial anthropology and the psychedelic sequence can be diagramed as shown opposite:

Up to this point we have noted Grof's empirical findings, and compared the way they fit into his Rank-extended psychiatric theories on the one hand and into the primordial understanding of man on the other. It remains to point out how the findings of seventeen years affected his own thinking.

Engaged as he was in "the first mapping of completely unknown territories" (U267), he could not have foreseen where his inquiry would lead. What he found was that in "the most fascinating intellectual and spiritual adventure of my life [it] opened up new fantastic areas and forced me to break with the old systems and frameworks" (U250). The first change in his thinking has already

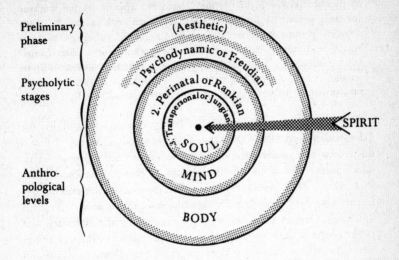

been noted: the psycholytic sequences showed the birth trauma to have more dynamic consequences than Grof and his strictly Freudian associates had supposed. This change psychoanalysis could accommodate, but not the one that followed. "I started my LSD research in 1956 as a convinced and dedicated psychoanalyst," he writes. "In the light of everyday clinical observations in LSD sessions, I found this conception untenable" (p. 17). Basically, what proved to be untenable was "the present . . . gloomy . . . image of man, which is to a great extent influenced by psychoanalysis" (U382).[7]

This picture of man,

> that of a social animal basically governed by blind and irrational instinctual forces . . . contradicts the experiences from the LSD sessions or at least appears superficial and limited. Most of the instinctual tendencies described by psychoanalysis (incestuous and murderous wishes, cannibalistic impulses, sadomasochistic inclinations, coprophilia, etc.) are very striking in the early LSD sessions; these observations are so common that they could almost be con-

7. The flyleaf of Rank's book which served as almost the bible for Grof's work in one of its stages carries a quotation from Nietzsche: "The very best . . . is, not to be born. . . . The next best . . . is . . . to die soon."

sidered experimental evidence for some of the basic assumptions of psychoanalysis. Most of them, however, appear in the sessions for only a limited period of time. This whole area can be transcended [whereupon] we are confronted with an image of man which is diametrically opposed to the previous one. Man in his innermost nature appears then as a being that is fundamentally in harmony with his environment and is governed by intrinsic high and universal values. [U382–83, deletions not indicated.]

This change in anthropology has been the solid effect of psychedelic evidence on Grof's thinking. In psychoanalytic terms, if Freud discovered the importance of infantile experience on ontogenetic development and Rank the importance of the experience of birth itself, Grof's discoveries carry this search for ever earlier etiologies—in psychoanalytic theory earlier = stronger—to its absolute limit: his optimistic view of man derives from discovering the influence and latent power of early-gestation memories; memories of the way things were when the womb was still uncongested and all was well. Beyond this revised anthropology, however, Grof has toyed with a changed ontology as well. Endowments that supplement his psychiatric competences have helped him here: he has an "ear" for metaphysics and an abiding ontological interest. These caused him to listen attentively from the start to his subjects' reports on the nature of reality, and in one of his recent papers, "LSD and the Cosmic Game: Outline of Psychedelic Cosmology and Ontology" (see footnote 3, page 156), he gives these reports full rein. Laying aside for the interval his role as research psychiatrist, which required seeing patients' experiences as shaped by if not projected from early formative experiences, in this paper Grof turns phenomenologist and allows their reports to stand in their own right. The view of reality that results is so uncannily like the one that has been outlined in this book that, interlacing paraphrases of passages in Grof's article with direct quotations from it, we present it here in summary.

The ultimate source of existence is the Void, the supracosmic Silence, the uncreated and absolutely ineffable Supreme.

The first possible formulation of this source is Universal Mind. Here, too, words fail, for Mind transcends the dichotomies, polarities, and paradoxes that harry the relative world. Insofar as description is attempted, the Vedantic ternary—Infinite Existence, Infinite Intelligence, Infinite Bliss—is as adequate as any.

God is not limited to his foregoing, "abstract" modes. He can be encountered concretely, as the God of the Old and New Testaments, Buddha, Shiva, or in other modes. These modes do not, however, wear the mantle of ultimacy or provide answers that are final.

The phenomenal worlds owe their existence to Universal Mind, which Mind does not itself become implicated in their categories. Man, together with the three-dimensional world he experiences, is but one of innumerable modes through which Mind experiences itself. The "heavy physicality" and seemingly objective finality of man's material world, its space-time grid and laws of nature that offer themselves as if they were *sine qua nons* of existence itself —all these are in fact highly provisional and relative. Under exceptional circumstances man can rise to a level of consciousness where he sees that taken together they constitute but one of inumerable sets of limiting constructs Universal Mind assumes. To saddle that Mind itself with these categories would be as ridiculous as trying to understand the human mind through the rules of chess.

Created entities tend progressively to lose contact with their original source and the awareness of their pristine identity with it. In the initial stage of this falling away, created entities maintain contact with their source and the separation is playful, relative, and obviously tentative. An image that would illustrate this stage is that of waves on the ocean. From a certain point of view they are individual entities; we can speak of a large, fast, green, and foamy wave, for example. At the same time it is transparently evident that in spite of its relative individuation the wave is part of the ocean.

At the next stage created entities assume a partial independence and we can observe the beginnings of "cosmic screenwork." Here unity with the source can be temporarily forgotten in the way an actor on stage can virtually forget his own identity while he identifies with the character he portrays.

Continuation of the process of partitioning results in a situation in which individuation is permanently and for all practical purposes complete, and only occasionally do intimations of the original wholeness resurface. This can be illustrated by the relationship between cells of a body, organs, and the body as a whole. Cells are separate entities but function as parts of organs. The latter have even more independence, but they too play out their roles in the complete organism. Individuation and participation are dialectically combined. Complex biochemical interactions bridge provisional boundaries to ensure the functioning of the organism as a whole.

In the final stage the separation is practically complete. Liaison with the source is lost and the original identity completely forgotten. The "screen" is now all but impermeable; radical qualitative change is required for the original unity to be restored. Symbol of this might be a snowflake, crystallized from water that has evaporated from the ocean. It bears little outward similarity to its source and must undergo a change in structure if reunion is to occur.

Human beings who manage to effect the change just referred to find thereafter that life's polarities paradoxically both do and do not exist. This holds for such contraries as spirit/matter, good/evil, stability/motion, heaven/hell, beauty/ugliness, agony/ecstasy, etc. In the last analysis there is no difference between subject and object, observer and observed, experiencer and experienced, creator and creation.

In the early years of psychoanalysis when hostility was shown to its reports and theories on account of their astonishing novelty, and they were dismissed as products of their authors' perverted imaginations, Freud used to hold up against this objection the argument that no human brain could have invented such facts and connections had they not been persistently forced on it by a series of converging and interlocking observations. Grof might have argued equally: to wit, that the "psychedelic cosmology and ontology" that his patients came up with is as uninventable as Freud's own system. In fact, however, he does not do so. In the manner of a good phenomenologist he lets the picture speak for itself, neither belittling it by referring it back to causes that in purporting to explain it would explain it away, nor arguing that it is true. As phenomenologists themselves would say, he "brackets" his own judgment regarding the truth question and contents himself with reporting what his patients said about it.

The idea that the "three-dimensional world" is only one of many experiential worlds created by the Universal Mind . . . appeared to them much more logical than the opposite alternative that is so frequently taken for granted, namely, that the material world has objective reality of its own and that the human consciousness and the concept of God are merely products of highly organized matter, the human brain. When closely analyzed the latter concept presents at least as many incongruences, paradoxes and absurdities as the described concept of the Universal Mind. The problems of finity versus infinity of time and space; the enigma of the origin of matter, energy and space; and the mystery of the prime impulse appear to be so overwhelming and defeating that one seriously questions why this approach should be given priority in our thinking. [p. 11]

Index